HISTORIC WISCONSIN ROADSIDES

BY TOM MANUS & KRISTI FLICK MANUS

REEDY PRESS

DEDICATION

Timothy, you are our whole world. We are so proud of you and love you so much.

—Mom and Dad

Reedy Press
PO Box 5131
St. Louis, MO 63139
reedypress.com

Book Design: Julie Sturma

Photos courtesy of Tom Manus and Kristi Flick Manus unless otherwise noted.

Library of Congress Control Number: 2024949612

ISBN: 9781681065809

26 27 28 29 5 4 3 2

CONTENTS

INTRODUCTION:

BUCKLE UP, BUTTERCUP:

Hit the Road with *Historic Wisconsin Roadsides*

Dust off your maps, gas up the tank, and prepare to rediscover the Badger State! *Historic Wisconsin Roadsides* isn't just a road trip guide; it's a time machine disguised as a roadmap. Join authors and history buffs Tom and Kristi Manus as you navigate enchanting backroads, explore hidden historical gems, and uncover stories etched into the very fabric of Wisconsin. Find new experiences for a lifetime of memories.

- **Experience small-town charm:** Discover small towns for unique attractions, profound history, expressive culture, and celebrated heritage.
- **Step back in time:** Visit living history museums, restored villages, and quirky roadside attractions that bring the past to life.
- **Indulge in local flavor:** Sample traditional dishes, meet passionate artisans, and discover unique shops hidden off the beaten path.
- **Connect with the land and water:** Glide along the Mississippi's ever-changing curves, meander through harbor villages on the coasts of the Great Lakes, taste pure freedom cruising the hills of the Driftless Region, and marvel at breathtaking natural wonders that have shaped Wisconsin's history.

Whether you're a history buff, a lover of culture, or simply looking for a unique adventure, *Historic Wisconsin Roadsides* offers:

- **Detailed itineraries:** Choose from themed road trips such as "The Yellowstone Trail and the Great River Road," "Madison and Heritage Towns," "White Arrow Signs," and "Harbor Towns and Shipwrecks," or create your own with the book's comprehensive listings.

- **Vivid storytelling:** Immerse yourself in the past with captivating narratives that bring history to life.
- **Stunning photography:** Get a visual taste of the journey with beautiful color photographs that capture the essence of Wisconsin.
- **Practical information:** Find insider tips on accommodation, restaurants, hidden gems, and things to do, ensuring a smooth and unforgettable trip.

So grab your copy of *Historic Wisconsin Roadsides*, pack your sense of adventure, and get ready to embark on a journey that will leave you saying, "You betcha!" This book isn't just a road trip; it's a love letter to Wisconsin's rich history, captivating spirit, and the hidden stories waiting to be discovered. Are you ready to answer the call of the open road?

LAKE SUPERIOR
DULUTH
SUPERIOR
WASHBURN
APOSTLE ISLANDS
ASHLAND
IRONWOOD
CHEQUAMEGON NATIONAL FOREST
MERCER
LAND O' LAKES
LAC DU FLAMBEAU
ST. GERMAIN
EAGLE RIVER
MINOCQUA
NICOLET NATIONAL FOREST
KINSFORD
PHILLIPS
RHINELANDER
DANBURY
HAYWARD
SPOONER
CAMERON
LADYSMITH
NEW RICHMOND
MEDFORD
MERRILL
ANTIGO
WISCONSIN
CHIPPEWA FALLS
MENOMONIE
EAU CLAIRE
OCONTO FALLS
SHAWANO
CLINTONVILLE
MARSHFIELD
STEVENS POINT
MONDOVI
NEILLSVILLE
WHITEHALL
WISCONSIN RAPIDS
WAUPACA
APPLETON
BLACK RIVER FALLS
PETENWELL DAM
MISSISSIPPI RIVER
WAUTOMA
TOMAH
CASTLE ROCK LAKE
OSHKOSH
LA CROSSE
NEW LISBON
WESTBY
PORTAGE
BEAVER DAM
WEST BEND
RICHLAND CENTER
IOWA
MENOMONEE FALLS
BOSCOBEL
LAKE MENDOTA
MADISON
STOUGHTON
DODGEVILLE
LANCASTER
JANESVILLE
MONROE
DUBUQUE
ILLINOIS

WHITE ARROW SIGNS

UP NORTH: VACATIONING IN WHITE ARROW SIGNS

Wisconsinites have a deep-rooted love affair with the Northwoods, a passion often expressed through their unwavering desire to spend time in cabins and lodges. This "up north" culture is a cherished part of our state's identity, fueled by lake life, outdoor recreation, and a sense of nostalgia.

The Northwoods starkly contrasts with the hustle and bustle of urban life. White arrow signs point to rustic retreats that offer a sense of home away from home, where memories are made and traditions are passed down from generation to generation. For many Wisconsinites, spending time up north is a cherished family tradition. Generations of families have gathered at cabins and lodges, creating lasting memories and strengthening bonds.

The allure of the Northwoods lies not only in its natural beauty but also in its ability to evoke a sense of nostalgia. The quiet solitude, combined with the familiar sounds of nature, can transport us back to simpler times. It's a place where we can disconnect from the distractions of modern life and reconnect with what truly matters.

One of the most recognized symbols of the Northwoods, Claire d'Loon, stands tall in Mercer. The giant fiberglass sculpture is a popular spot for photos and represents Wisconsin's love for the aquatic bird, and its wail heard echoing across lakes. Likewise, colorful boathouses line the picturesque shoreline of Lake Minocqua. These historic structures offer a glimpse into the Northwoods' boating heritage.

Pack your bags—roadside attractions, nostalgia, and the open road await!

TO START THE TOUR, BEGIN IN FLORENCE and drive through the heart of Wisconsin's "up north" resort culture and end in Phillips.

Walk through the many exhibits at the Wild Rivers Interpretive Center.

FLORENCE

Florence County is synonymous with pristine wilderness, and it is the core of Wisconsin's Wild River country. The county is home to two of the original state-designated Wild Rivers: the Pine and the Popple. With their untamed beauty and challenging class III rapids, these rivers have drawn outdoor enthusiasts for generations. The "Wild" designation signifies undeveloped shorelines and commitment to preserving the river's natural state. Paddlers of all skill levels can find adventure on these rivers, using numerous access points. From the Pine River's exhilarating rapids to the Popple's serene stretches, there's something for everyone.

Beyond the rivers, Florence County boasts a rich tapestry of natural wonders. With their spectacular beauty, waterfalls like Breakwater Falls and Little Bull Falls add to the region's allure. Hiking trails wind through ancient forests, offering glimpses of wildlife and breathtaking vistas.

The Florence County Wild Rivers Interpretive Center is a treasure trove of knowledge, providing valuable insights into the area's history, ecology, and recreational opportunities. Visitors can learn about the region's logging heritage, the importance of conservation, and the best ways to explore the wild rivers.

Whether you're an experienced paddler, a hiker seeking solitude, or simply someone who appreciates the beauty of nature, Florence County delivers an unforgettable experience. Its wild rivers and pristine landscapes inspire and captivate those who venture into its embrace.

Phone home from downtown Florence, retro style.

Visit!

FLORENCE COUNTY WILD RIVERS INTERPRETIVE CENTER
5638 Forestry Dr.
715-528-4464

LASALLE FALLS TRAILHEAD
2733 La Salle Falls Access Rd.
Eighteen Foot Falls
18 Foot Falls Rd., Pembine

TWELVE FOOT FALLS PARK
12 Foot Falls Rd., Dunbar

Eat!

ANNIE'S TRADING POST
5203 Keyes Lake Dr.
715-528-2170

BARB'S CAFÉ
633 Central Ave.
715-528-4219

MICHAELA MAY'S BAKERY
308 Central Ave.
906-282-3027

CHUCKWAGON RESTAURANT
1438 FDR Ln.

to Do!

THE PARTY FIDDLE FACTORY
4666 First Crossing Rd.
715-528-4209

KEYES PEAK SKI HILL
4960 WI-101
715-528-3228

SPREAD EAGLE BARRENS STATE NATURAL AREA
West Ellwood Lake Rd.
715-528-5377

TIP

Florence's Crafters on Central studio offers a variety of art workshops for all ages, from painting to pottery. It's a great place to unleash creativity or learn new skills.

Stay!

LAKESIDE BED & BREAKFAST
509 Furnace St.
715-528-3259

CAMPING IN THE CLOUDS
4080 US-2
715-528-5596

BORREMANS LAKE HOUSE
4999 Cal's Lane
920-619-6140

FROM FLORENCE, follow WI-70 W, then turn right onto WI-139 N/ WI-70 W/WI-70 Trunk W. Turn left onto WI-70 W. Continue on WI-70 W into Eagle River.

EAGLE RIVER

The iconic white signs marking the entrance to "Up North" Wisconsin have become synonymous with relaxation, recreation, and escape. While their exact origins are shrouded in local lore, their history parallels the development of Eagle River and the surrounding region.

Eagle River, the heart of the Northwoods, has a history that dates back to the early 1800s. Originally inhabited by Native American tribes, the area transformed with the arrival of European settlers in the mid-19th century. Drawn by the promise of abundant timber, these pioneers carved out a living in the rugged wilderness.

In the early 20th century, as the lumber industry declined, the region began rediscovering its appealing outdoors. With the abundance of lakes, the Northwoods offered an idyllic escape from the stresses of urban life. This growing popularity led to a surge in tourism, and the need for clear signage became apparent. With their practicality and easy visibility in the forests, the white "up north" signs emerged as a solution that visitors and locals alike could appreciate.

to Do!

EAGLE RIVER CITY BEACH
932 Silver Lake Rd.
715-479-9634

ARROW GIFT SHOP
201 E Wall St.
715-479-4903

THE WAREHOUSE ART CENTER
107 S Railroad St.
715-479-4060

Visit!

WORLD SNOWMOBILE HEADQUARTERS
1521 N Railroad St.
715-479-2186

TREES FOR TOMORROW
519 E Sheridan St.
715-479-6456

Shop where your grandparents did at Arrow Gift Shop.

Grab a dog at House of Dogs.

TIP

Charles Comiskey, the legendary owner of the Chicago White Sox, spent his final years in Eagle River. He owned a lodge, which he affectionately named Home Plate, where he died in 1931.

The signs served as welcoming beacons for visitors, their white color standing out against the lush greenery, guiding them to the region's numerous resorts, restaurants, and attractions. As the region's reputation as a vacation destination grew, so did the iconic signs. Today, they are more than just directional markers; they represent a way of life, a state of mind, and an integral part of the Northwoods experience.

Eat!

CHANTICLEER INN
1458 E Dollar Lake Rd.
715-479-4486

FRIENDSHIP HOUSE FAMILY RESTAURANT
101 W Wall St.
715-479-1070

PINE ISLE LODGE
1261 Pine Isle Rd.
Three Lakes
715-546-3333

EDDIE B'S WHITE SPRUCE RESTAURANT & TAVERN
419 N Railroad St.
715-480-4000

HOUSE OF DOGS
418 E Wall St.
715-477-1949

GREENHILL'S LOG CABIN
226 US-45, Conover
715-479-2787

Stay!

EDGEWATER INN & COTTAGES
5054 WI-70 West
715-479-4011

EAGLE WATERS RESORT
3958 Eagle Waters Rd.
715-479-4411

JENSEN'S EAGLE LAKE RESORT
1800 Eagle Park Ln.
715-479-8177

A1 GYPSY VILLA RESORT
938 Gypsy Villa Ln.
715-479-8644

LEAVING EAGLE RIVER, head south on US-45 S. Turn right onto County Highway A/Superior Street. Turn left onto WI-17 S and follow into Rhinelander.

Step back in time at the lumberjack's cook shanty in Pioneer Park Historical Complex.

RHINELANDER

Rhinelander's story is deeply rooted in the rugged wilderness of northern Wisconsin. In the late 19th century, Rhinelander was a hub of activity as a lumber town, with towering pines being transformed into building materials that shaped the nation. Railroads brought in workers and transported lumber to markets across the country. The city's growth and prosperity were closely associated with the rise and fall of the timber industry. The town thrived on the industry, but the relentless pace of logging eventually depleted the forests.

Rhinelander then reinvented itself as a thriving tourist destination. Visitors flock to the area to experience the abundant resorts, "up north" feel, and nature. Outdoor enthusiasts find paradise in fishing, boating, hiking, and snowmobiling. Its natural beauty, with countless pristine lakes, dense forests, and wildlife, draws visitors year-round.

The city's cultural scene reflects its heritage. The Hodag, a mythical creature said to inhabit the area, has become a beloved local mascot. The Hodag Festival, held annually, celebrates Rhinelander's unrivaled identity.

A visit to Rhinelander is an opportunity to experience the authentic charm of the Northwoods. You can still hear the echoes of the logger era in local folklore and historic buildings around Rhinelander. Whether exploring the great outdoors, discovering the city's history, or immersing yourself in local culture, there's something everyone can enjoy in this welcoming community.

TIP

Eugene Shepard is the mastermind behind the Hodag legend. With a knack for storytelling, he fabricated the creature in 1893. This clever hoax is an integral part of Rhinelander's identity.

Eat!

RHINELANDER BREWING COMPANY
43 Brown St.
715-550-2337

NORTHWESTERN HOTEL LOUNGE
119 S Brown St.
715-362-5080

FIRESIDE SUPPER CLUB
6012 Co. Rd. K
715-369-4717

RHINELANDER CAFÉ & PUB
33 N Brown St.
715-362-2918

Stay!

FISHER'S RESORT, BAR & GRILL
4225 W Lake George Rd.
715-362-3691

CLEAR LAKE INN AND RESORT
4475 Co. Rd. P
406-431-3973

PINE VALLEY LODGE
3980 Lakeshore Dr.
608-937-9626

MERRY DALE RESORT
4149 Satuit Ln.
715-828-0195

Visit!

PIONEER PARK HISTORICAL COMPLEX
Martin Lynch Dr.
715-369-5004

HOLMBOE CONIFER FOREST
Boyce Dr.

WASHBURN LAKE SILENT SPORTS TRAILS AREA
County Park Rd.

to Do!

KOVAC PLANETARIUM
2392 Mud Creek Rd.
715-490-6956

ARTSTART, INC.
68 S Stevens St.
715-362-4328

HODAG WATER SHOWS, INC.
Hodag Park
509 Hodag Park Dr.

MEL'S TRADING POST
105 S Brown St.
715-362-5800

HEAD NORTH from Rhinelander on WI-47 N. Turn left on Midlake Road. Turn right on Country Club Road. Turn right onto US-51 N into Minocqua.

Train depot at Pioneer Park Historical Complex

MINOCQUA

The historic boathouses of Minocqua are architectural landmarks that are integral to the town's identity and development. These structures, often opulent and meticulously crafted, were symbols of wealth and leisure in the early 20th century. As affluent individuals from Chicago and other urban centers discovered the allure of Minocqua's pristine lakes, they didn't just build elaborate boathouses; they transformed the town. These structures, serving as practical storage for watercraft, also became social hubs, hosting lavish parties and gatherings. This influx of wealth contributed to Minocqua's economic growth and fundamentally transformed it from a quiet fishing village into a thriving resort town.

The architectural diversity and blend of styles of these boathouses is a reflection of Minocqua's unique charm. From rustic log cabins to grand Victorian-style structures, Minocqua's lakeshore boasts a captivating array of architectural styles. Most Minocqua boathouses have spartan second-story living quarters, but some, like the iconic red Coys' Eagles Nest with its corner tower, offer more elaborate upper levels. This richness of these boathouses is a draw for tourists and a novel feature that sets Minocqua apart.

Preserving these historic boathouses has played a crucial role in maintaining Minocqua's heritage. Many of these structures have been carefully restored, ensuring that future generations can appreciate their architectural significance.

Today, Minocqua's boathouses are iconic symbols of the town's legacy. They remind visitors of the area's golden age and contribute to its enduring appeal as a premier vacation destination.

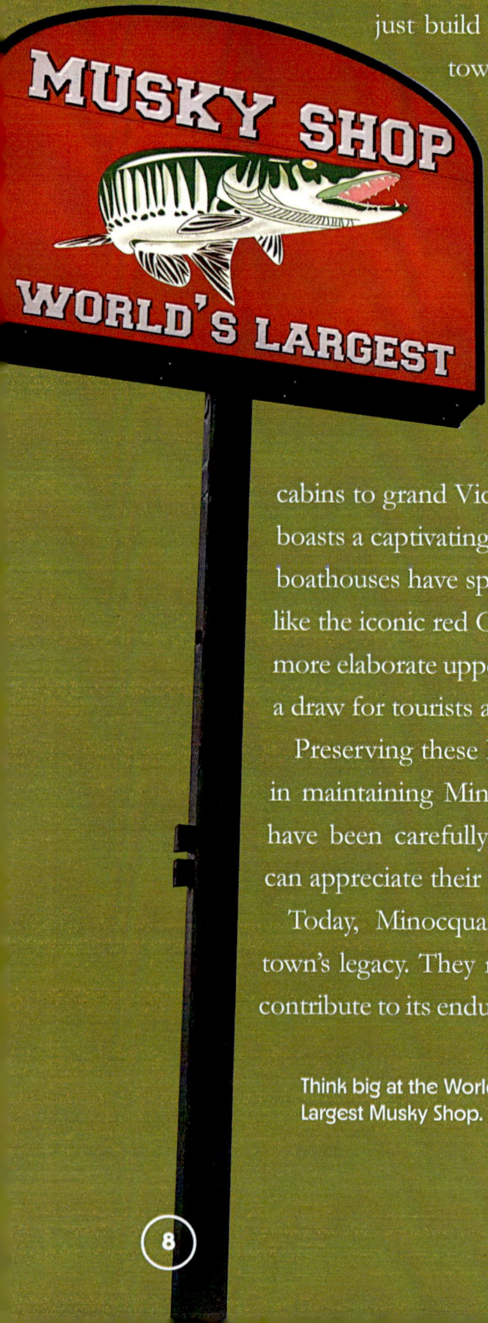

Think big at the World's Largest Musky Shop.

Eat!

NORWOOD PINES SUPPER CLUB
10171 WI-70
715-356-3666

HOGGIE DOGGIE'S
8803 Hwy. 47, Woodruff
715-356-5938

Visit!

TORPY PARK
806 US-51

RED CROWN LODGE
3852 US-51, Woodruff
715-385-2709

MIN-AQUA BATS WATER SKI SHOW
422 W Park Ave.
715-255-0636

NORTHWOODS WILDLIFE CENTER
8683 S Blumenstein Rd.
715-356-7400

ROLLIE & HELEN'S MUSKY SHOP
7542 US-51
715-356-6011

WORLD'S LARGEST PENNY
820 Third Ave., Woodruff

TIP

Elizabeth Taylor had a significant connection to Minocqua. As a teenager, she spent many summers visiting her uncle, Howard Young, an art dealer who lived on Lake Minocqua.

Stay!

BLACK'S CLIFF RESORT
10223 Lower Kaubashine Rd., Hazelhurst
715-356-3018

EAGLE SHORES RESORT
6119 Co. Rd. Y
Hazelhurst
715-356-5329

to Do!

DAN'S MINOCQUA FUDGE
521 Oneida St.
715-356-2662

WILDWOOD WILDLIFE PARK ZOO & SAFARI
10094 WI-70
715-356-5588

SCHEER'S LUMBERJACK SHOWS
1126 First Ave., Woodruff
715-356-4050

BEARSKIN STATE TRAILHEAD PARK
Across from the Post Office at 126 Front St.

DR. KATE MUSEUM
923 Second Ave.
Woodruff
715-356-6896

Classic boats at Torpy Park in Minocqua

FROM MINOCQUA, take US-51 N and turn right onto County Highway J. Turn right onto WI-47 S. Turn left onto Woodruff Road. Turn right onto Hatchery Road/ Woodruff Road. Turn right on Townline Road. Turn left onto WI-70 W.

ST. GERMAIN

St. Germain is renowned for its vintage resorts, blending old-world charm and modern comfort. These historic establishments complement the area's rich history as a sought-after vacation destination.

Built in the early to mid-20th century, these resorts were designed to cater to visitors seeking respite from the bustling city. Their architecture often reflects the rustic beauty of the Northwoods, with log cabins, stone fireplaces, and spacious porches. Many of these resorts have been lovingly restored, preserving their historic character while incorporating contemporary amenities.

Guests staying at a vintage resort in St. Germain can expect a truly authentic Northwoods experience. Imagine waking up to the sound of loons, enjoying a good book on a sun-drenched porch, and spending the day exploring the area's serene beauty. These resorts, with their variety of activities such as boating, fishing, and hiking, are ideal for families and couples alike.

Beyond their accommodations, vintage resorts in St. Germain often have a rich history to share. Tales of famous guests, local legends, and bygone eras can be heard from long-time staff members. Staying at one of these historic properties is an opportunity to immerse yourself in the rich tapestry of the Northwoods.

TIP

Awassa Nature Preserve has many trails worth hiking, especially for beginners. These trails are great for those looking for a less strenuous walk, are wheelchair accessible, and are dog friendly.

Snowmobile Hall of Fame

PITLIK'S SAND BEACH RESORT
4833 Sand Beach Dr., Eagle River
833-748-5457

MCGREGOR'S BLINK BONNIE SUPPER CLUB
1506 Jerry Rd.
715-542-3678

CLEARVIEW SUPPER CLUB
8599 Big St. Germain Dr.
715-542-3474

THE TIMBERS BAR AND GRILL
1053 Elbert Rd.
715-479-3059

McGregor's Blink Bonnie Supper Club: a Northwoods staple

JACKSON'S LAKESIDE COTTAGES
1180 Jackson Ln.
715-479-8640

FATH'S BIG WOODS RESORT
1640 Hwy. C
715-542-3865

HEELER'S QUIET COMFORT CABINS
8087 Lost Lake Dr. N
920-901-0803

WHISPERING PINE LODGE
8440 Pinewood Dr.
715-479-4828

SNOWMOBILE HALL OF FAME
1246 Sled World Blvd.
715-542-4463

BEAR PAW POTTERY
9020 Co. Rd. O
715-892-2143

SUTTER'S GOLD 'N FLEECE
9094 Co. Rd. O
715-479-7634

HAMMOCK HUT
330 WI-70
715-347-7467

HAWK'S NEST OUTFITTERS
6141 WI-70, Eagle River
715-479-7944

PLUM SKI-TERS WATER SKI SHOW
3230 State House Point Rd., Sayner
262-423-7586

LAKE NOKOMIS CRANBERRIES
6041 Co. Rd. D
Eagle River
715-479-6546 ext. 1007

FROM ST. GERMAIN, drive north on WI-70. Turn left onto County Highway N/Lake Street. Turn right onto County Highway M. Turn left onto North Creek Road. Turn left onto County Highway H. Turn right onto US-51 N and continue into Mercer.

MERCER

The Turtle-Flambeau Flowage is the heart and soul of Mercer. Created in 1926 by the Chippewa and Flambeau Improvement Company, this vast reservoir changed the landscape and the region's economic dynamics, shifting it from a primarily lumber-based economy to a vibrant tourism-driven one.

Before the flowage, the area was a mix of forests and smaller lakes. Logging was a significant industry in the area, and the potential for tourism could have been improved. The creation of the flowage dramatically changed this. Thousands of acres were inundated, creating a sprawling body of water with countless islands, bays, and inlets.

As the flowage took shape, it became apparent that this new aquatic playground held immense tourism potential. With their foresight and determination, early entrepreneurs recognized the opportunity and built

A souvenir staple in Mercer

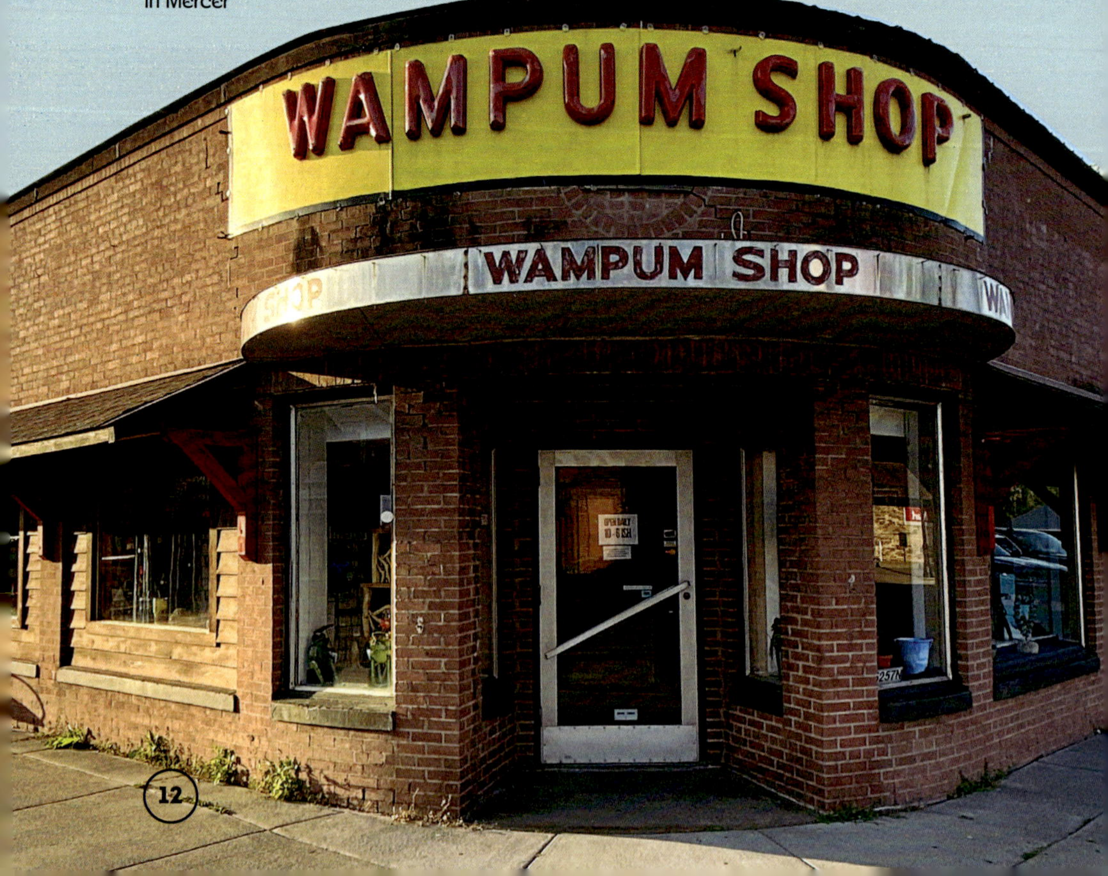

resorts, cabins, and campgrounds to accommodate visitors. Fishing, boating, and vacationing became popular pastimes. The area's captivating scenery and abundant wildlife drew people from across the state and beyond.

Over the decades, tourism has continued to grow, making the Turtle-Flambeau Flowage a significant economic driver for Mercer and the surrounding area. Today, visitors flock to the region to enjoy a variety of water sports, fishing, and simply relaxing on the shore.

The Turtle-Flambeau Flowage is a living, breathing entity that has shaped the region's history, economy, and culture.

Eat!

PINES RESTAURANT AND BEER GARDEN
5234 US-51
715-476-2933

TOM'S COUNTRY CAFÉ
5233 US-51
715-476-2433

ULLMAN'S DING-A-LING SUPPER CLUB
1711 US-51
715-476-2270

Stay!

CRANBERRY INN
5491 US-51
715-721-4700

JOE MILLER'S COTTAGES
6600 W Miller Rd.
Butternut
715-476-2505

BALSAM RIDGE LODGING
5910 Co. Hwy. FF
715-252-3144

DEADHORSE LODGE
4125 N Popko Cir. W
715-544-5851

Visit!

LAKE OF THE FALLS COUNTY PARK
4720 Co. Park Rd.
715-329-0826

POTATO RIVER FALLS
Potato River Rd.
Gurney
715-561-2922

RICE LAKE FALLS
Rice Lake Dr.
Claire d'Loon
5135 US-51

to Do!

LITTLE FINLAND
5750 US-2, Hurley
715-561-4360

MERCER DEPOT MUSEUM
5259 Lakeview Ave.
715-476-2216

WAMPUM SHOP
5257 Lakeview Ave.
715-476-2465

FEDERICO ROYAL BAKERY
5126 US-51
715-476-2800

TIP

Ralph Capone, Al Capone's brother and a lover of the Mercer area, built a house in 1942 and managed the Rex Hotel and Billy's Bar until he died in 1974.

Clair d'Loon. It's not the world's largest loon, but it's close.

FROM MERCER, follow US-51 S. Turn right onto WI-182 W/WI-47 S. Continue to follow WI-47 S into Lac Du Flambeau.

LAC DU FLAMBEAU

Lac du Flambeau, meaning "Lake of the Torches," has a history as deep as its surrounding waters. Initially inhabited by the Ojibwe people, the area was a hub for fishing and gathering. The name itself refers to the tribe's nighttime fishing practices using torches.

The arrival of European settlers in the 19th century marked a significant shift. The region's abundant timber resources drew loggers, transforming the landscape and economy. However, with the decline of the lumber industry, Lac du Flambeau began to focus on its natural beauty and recreational potential. Tourism emerged as a cornerstone of the local economy. The area's lakes, forests, and abundant wildlife proved irresistible to outdoor enthusiasts. Resorts and cabins began springing up, catering to visitors seeking respite from urban life. Fishing, boating, and hunting became popular attractions.

Today, Lac du Flambeau is a community that balances its rich heritage with modern challenges and opportunities. The Lac du Flambeau Band of Lake Superior Chippewa plays a significant role in the area's governance and economic development. They operate several successful businesses, including a casino, golf course, and resort.

Beyond its unspoiled nature, Lac du Flambeau is rich in cultural heritage. The Lac du Flambeau Reservation is home to a community that maintains its traditions while embracing modern life. Visitors can experience Ojibwe culture through art, music, and traditional ceremonies.

The combination of peaceful surroundings, cultural richness, and recreational opportunities makes Lac du Flambeau a unique and unforgettable destination.

TIP

The Lac du Flambeau Government Boarding School, operating from 1895 to 1932, forcibly removed Native American children from their homes, imposing Western culture while suppressing their language, culture, and traditions.

Eat!

LAKE PLACID INN
1520 Co. Rd. F, Minocqua
715-356-4202

RUSTIC PINES PUB
11758 WI-70, Minocqua
715-356-0038

HARRISON'S PUB & GRILL
3160 Pokegama Lake Trail
715-588-1811

Stay!

BIRCH TRAIL RESORT
8820 W Squaw Lake Rd.
715-588-1962

BUCKSKIN LAKE RESORT
14547 Buckskin Resort Dr.
715-356-3178

THOMSEN'S THUNDERBIRD HILL RESORT
2181 Co. Rd. D
715-588-7284

LAKE OF THE TORCHES RESORT CASINO
510 Old Abe Rd.
800-258-6724

ZELM'S WHITE SAND LAKE RESORT
3345 Sand Lake Lodge Ln.
715-588-3828

to Do!

WAASWAAGANING INDIAN BOWL-POW WOW
603 Peace Pipe Rd.
715-588-4252

GEORGE W. BROWN JR. OJIBWE MUSEUM & CULTURAL CENTER
603 Peace Pipe Rd.
715-588-3333

SPIRIT BERRY LLC
591 Peace Pipe Rd.
715-892-0906

Visit!

WILLIAM J. POUPART SR. FISH HATCHERY
2500 WI-47
715-588-2170

GOVERNMENT BOARDING SCHOOL AT LAC DU FLAMBEAU
828 Old Abe Rd.

FROM LAC DU FLAMBEAU, take Peace Pipe Road south. Turn right onto WI-70 W. Turn left onto Sheep Ranch Road. Turn right to stay on Sheep Ranch Road and enter Phillips.

Waaswaanaganing Indian Bowl Powwow

PHILLIPS

Fred Smith's life story is intricately woven into the fabric of Phillips, a town deeply marked by the lumber industry. Born in 1886 to German immigrant parents, Smith grew up immersed in the rugged world of the Northwoods. Like many young men of his generation, he found employment in the booming lumber industry.

Folk art at the Wisconsin Concrete Park

The late 19th and early 20th centuries were a golden age for logging in Wisconsin. Vast forests of pine and hardwood trees provided the raw material for a burgeoning nation. Phillips, strategically located amidst these timber riches, thrived as a lumber town. In this environment, Smith developed a deep connection to the woods and the men who worked them. However, the relentless pace of logging took its toll. Arthritis forced Smith to retire from the lumber industry in 1948. He then embarked on an extraordinary artistic journey. With no formal training, he began sculpting life-sized and larger-than-life concrete figures on his property.

Smith's sculptures reflect his life experiences. Many of his works depict scenes from the lumber era, capturing the spirit of the hardworking men who shaped the region. His concrete figures, though rough-hewn, convey a powerful sense of the lumberjacks' physicality and determination, making the audience feel a deep connection to Phillips's history and the resilience and ingenuity of the town's people.

Hidden Cove Resort on Long Lake in Phillips

TIP

Timm's Hill boasts an observation tower offering stunning 30-mile Northwood views. Climb the stairs for panoramic vistas of Wisconsin's highest natural point at 1951.5 feet.

Eat!

NORTHWOODS SUPPER CLUB
N14066 Flambeau Ave.
715-762-4447

THE FILLING STATION
109 S Fifth St.
715-661-8539

Stay!

ROCK GARDEN TAVERN VACATION RENTAL
N8220 Hwy. 13
715-339-7282

HIDDEN VALLEY INN & RESORT
W7714 Co. Rd. W
715-820-1297

RUSTY'S LOON BAY RESORT
N8075 E Wilson Flowage Rd.
715-339-4638

HIDDEN COVE RESORT
W7396 S Long Lake Rd.
715-820-3881

CITY OF PHILLIPS' CHAIN-O-LAKES CAMPGROUND
Beach Rd.
715-339-3125

Visit!

FRED SMITH'S WISCONSIN CONCRETE PARK
N8236 State Hwy. 13
715-339-7282

TIMM'S HILL
W3206 Co. Rd. RR
715-339-6371

KNOX CREEK HERITAGE CENTER
N4517 W Knox Rd.
715-564-2525

SOLBERG LAKE COUNTY PARK
N10750 Co. Park Rd.
715-339-3742

to Do!

CHEQUAMEGON SMITH RAPIDS COVERED BRIDGE
Smith Rapids Rd.

ST. CROIX OF PARK FALLS
856 Fourth Ave. N
715-762-3226

SMITH LAKE COUNTY PARK
Omaha Rd.
715-339-6371

ROUND LAKE LOGGING DAM
N15296 Logging Dam Rd.
608-712-6479

LAKE SUPERIOR
APOSTLE ISLANDS
WASHBURN
ASHLAND
IRONWOOD
CHEQUAMEGON NATIONAL FOREST
MICHIGAN
MARQUETTE
LAND O' LAKES
EAGLE RIVER
NICOLET NATIONAL FOREST
KINSFORD
PARK FALLS
PHILLIPS
RHINELANDER
LADYSMITH
MERRILL
MEDFORD
ANTIGO
MARINETTE
GREEN BAY
WISCONSIN
OCONTO FALLS
STURGEON BAY
SHAWANO
CLINTONVILLE
MARSHFIELD
ALGOMA
GREEN BAY
STEVENS POINT
NEILLSVILLE
APPLETON
WAUPACA
WISCONSIN RAPIDS
HALL
BLACK RIVER FALLS
PETENWELL DAM
WAUTOMA
MANITOWOC-TWO RIVERS
OSHKOSH
LAKE WINNEBAGO
TOMAH
CASTLE ROCK LAKE
LA CROSSE
NEW LISBON
SHEBOYGAN
WESTBY
PORTAGE
PORT WASHINGTON
RICHLAND CENTER
CEDARBURG
BOSCOBEL
LAKE MENDOTA
MADISON
MILWAUKEE
STOUGHTON
DODGEVILLE
LANCASTER
RACINE
JANESVILLE
MONROE
KENOSHA
DUBUQUE
ILLINOIS

HARBOR TOWNS AND SHIPWRECKS

Embark on a captivating journey along Wisconsin's coastline, discovering diverse experiences from Kenosha to Algoma. Learn about maritime history, including numerous shipwrecks, nostalgic eateries, and cultural landmarks that have shaped this region.

One example is Kenosha, the southernmost city, with a charming downtown, historic museums, and a bustling harbor market. Enjoy a ride on historic streetcars or indulge in meals at its two classic drive-in restaurants and Franks Diner, a classic railcar-style eatery. Learn about the city's beginnings and industrial heritage at the Kenosha Public Museum. Or visit the Kenosha Light Station, a restored beacon that once guided ships into the harbor.

Sheboygan, another significant harbor town, boasts a variety of attractions. Visit the Wade House Historic Site, a restored stagecoach stop that provides a glimpse into the past. Plus, experience the magic of a Lake Michigan sunrise: stroll the beach at Kohler-Andrae State Park or admire the view from Blue Harbor Resort.

Manitowoc, a different type of harbor town, is home to the Wisconsin Maritime Museum and features the USS *Cobia*, a restored World War II submarine. You can learn about the city's shipbuilding heritage and the region's naval history.

Discover Manitowoc's shipbuilding history and Algoma's waterfront charm. Explore the Algoma Harbor, admire Walldog murals throughout town, and enjoy stunning lakefront views in this popular fishing destination. Satisfy your cravings at the quirky Smashed on the Rocks, or enjoy a glass of von Stiehl Winery wine.

TO START THE TOUR,

BEGIN IN KENOSHA
and drive along Lake Michigan and end in the Door Peninsula at Algoma.

KENOSHA

Kenosha features a transportation gem: a restored electric streetcar system that gives nostalgic rides through the city. The original streetcar system in Kenosha operated from 1903 to 1932, providing a vital mode of transportation.

In the late 1990s, Kenosha began restoring historic PCC streetcars and constructing a new track system. The goal was to create a vibrant downtown area and offer residents and tourists an extraordinary experience. Today, the Kenosha streetcar operates on a two-mile loop, providing scenic views of Lake Michigan, HarborPark, and the city's historic districts. The restored streetcars, each painted in a different city's livery, are modes of transportation and rolling museums, offering a glimpse into the past.

From the vintage charm of its streetcars to the haunting mysteries of its underwater world, Kenosha provides a diverse range of experiences. One of the most famous shipwrecks in the area is the SS *Wisconsin*. Launched in 1881, she was a marvel of engineering for her time, boasting an iron hull that was an affirmation to technological advancement.

Lake Michigan adventure
Courtesy of Tim Manus

Disaster struck on October 29, 1929, just days after the infamous Wall Street crash. Caught in a ferocious storm off the coast of Kenosha, the ship began to take on water rapidly. The wreck of the SS *Wisconsin* now rests upright on the lake bottom, approximately 130 feet below the surface. While the SS *Wisconsin* is undoubtedly the most renowned, it's far from the only vessel to find its final resting place near Kenosha.

TIP

The Italian American Club is a must-try culinary experience. Known for its top-notch food and generous portions, don't be surprised if you see patrons with Tupperware to take home leftovers.

Eat!

FRANKS DINER
508 58th St.
262-657-1017

THE COFFEE POT
4914 Seventh Ave.
262-653-8849

BIG STAR DRIVE-IN
1500 Washington Rd.
262-658-1572

THE SPOT DRIVE-IN
2117 75th St.
262-654-9294

OLIVER'S BAKERY
3526 Roosevelt Rd.
262-652-3984

Visit!

KENOSHA PUBLIC MUSEUM
5500 First Ave.
262-653-4140

KENOSHA HISTORY CENTER
220 51st Pl.
262-654-5770

DINOSAUR DISCOVERY MUSEUM
5608 10th Ave.
262-653-4450

DURKEE MANSION AT THE KEMPER CENTER
6501 Third Ave.
262-925-8040

Stay!

THE STELLA HOTEL & BALLROOM
5706 Eighth Ave.
262-842-2000

MERRY YACHT INN
4815 Seventh Ave.

THE COFFEE POT INN
4914 Seventh Ave.
262-653-8849

to Do!

HISTORIC ELECTRIC STREETCARS
Kenosha Transit Center
724 54th St.
262-653-4287

KENOSHA (SOUTHPORT) LIGHT STATION
5117 Fourth Ave.
262-654-5770

WASHINGTON PARK VELODROME
Washington Rd.

Jump off the streetcar for a stroll through Harbor Park.
Courtesy of Tim Manus

TRAVEL NORTH FROM KENOSHA on WI-32/Sheridan Road. Turn right on Washington Avenue, arriving in Racine.

The Firehouse 3 Museum

RACINE

The kringle, a flaky, buttery pastry filled with a variety of sweet fillings, is a treat with deep roots in European tradition. Its journey to becoming a Wisconsin staple is a story of immigration, culinary innovation, and enduring popularity.

Originating from Northern Europe, the kringle's history is intertwined with the pretzel. Introduced by Roman Catholic monks in the 13th century, pretzels evolved into sweet and savory pastries, including the kringle. Its name, derived from Old Norse, signifies "ring" or "circle," reflecting its characteristic shape.

The kringle found its way to the United States through Danish immigrants who settled in Racine in the late 19th century. These skilled bakers brought their cherished recipes, adapting them to local tastes and ingredients.

The heart of the kringle is its filling. Traditional flavors include almond, raspberry, cherry, and pecan, but modern variations have expanded the possibilities to include fruit, cream cheese, and chocolate. Bakers often add a sweet glaze or almond topping to complete the kringle, which enhances the pastry's flavor and visual appeal. Over time, the kringle evolved into the delectable pastry we know today, characterized by its delicate layers of dough, decadent fillings, and distinctive almond topping.

Racine has become synonymous with the kringle, which has garnered statewide and national recognition. In 2013, it was officially designated as the state pastry of Wisconsin, solidifying its place in the state's culinary heritage.

Eat!

HOBNOB
277 Sheridan Rd.
262-552-8008

KEWPEE SANDWICH SHOP
520 Wisconsin Ave.
262-634-9601

THE IVANHOE PUB & EATERY
231 Main St.
262-637-4730

OLDE MADRID
418 Sixth St.
262-619-0940

WELLS BROTHERS ITALIAN RESTAURANT
2148 Mead St.
262-632-4408

JOEY'S YARDARM
920 Erie St.
262-633-8270

LITTLEPORT BREWING COMPANY
214 Third St.
262-629-6976

Visit!

WINDPOINT LIGHTHOUSE
4725 Lighthouse Dr.
262-639-3777

FIREHOUSE 3 MUSEUM
700 Sixth St.

FIRST PRESBYTERIAN CHURCH UNDERGROUND RAILROAD TOUR
716 College Ave.
262-632-1686

MODINE-BENSTEAD OBSERVATORY AT THE RACINE ASTRONOMICAL SOCIETY
112 63rd Dr.
262-878-2774

BUCYRUS MUSEUM
1919 12th Ave.
414-671-3850

TIP

Racine's First Presbyterian Church is believed to have played a crucial role in the Underground Railroad. Free tours are offered to explore rumored escape tunnels.

to Do!

HOT SHOP GLASS
239 Wisconsin Ave.
262-833-0095

STAR ROLLER RINK
1825 Sycamore Ave.
262-633-1110

Stay!

HOTEL VERDANT
500 Main St.
262-456-6851

FROM RACINE, HEAD NORTH ON WI-32. Turn right onto South Pennsylvania Avenue. Use the left two lanes to turn left onto WI-794 N. Exit toward Port of Milwaukee. Turn right onto South Carferry Drive. Go straight on Access Road. Turn left on East Bay Street and right on WI-32 in Milwaukee's Harbor District.

Surround yourself with Kewpie dolls at Kewpee Sandwich Shop.

MILWAUKEE

Milwaukee's Harbor District, once a bustling industrial epicenter, has undergone a dramatic transformation. Its history is deeply connected with the city's growth as a major shipping and manufacturing center.

In the 19th century, as Milwaukee emerged as a thriving port city on Lake Michigan, the Harbor District became its beating heart. Warehouses, factories, and shipyards lined the waterfront, and the area was a hive of activity. The district played a crucial role in the city's economic prosperity, shipping goods across the Great Lakes and beyond.

In recent decades, a concerted effort has been made to revitalize the Harbor District. Abandoned warehouses have been transformed into trendy lofts and offices, and the waterfront has been redeveloped into a public space.

Barnacle Bud's, one of Milwaukee's most popular restaurants, is undoubtedly a Milwaukee treasure deserving of its spotlight. Situated on the Kinnickinnic River, this local eatery has carved out a unique niche as a waterfront oasis.

Barnacle Bud's story is one of organic growth and community-driven success. Originally a yacht club, the space was transformed into a casual hangout for boaters seeking respite from the water. Word of mouth quickly

Tenuta's Italian Restaurant

spread, drawing in a broader clientele eager to experience the laid-back atmosphere and delicious food.

Over the years, Barnacle Bud's has evolved into a local institution known for its outdoor patio, live music, and a menu catering to various tastes. Today, Barnacle Bud's remains a popular destination offering a taste of Milwaukee's waterfront culture.

TIP

At the Holler House, you can bowl at the oldest sanctioned bowling alley in the United States. Teenagers manually reset the wooden pins on the original wood lanes from 1910.

Eat!

BARNACLE BUD'S
1955 S Hilbert St.
414-481-9974

DON'S TV & REPAIR SPEAKEASY
1100 S First St.
414-808-0305

LEON'S FROZEN CUSTARD
3131 S 27th St.
414-383-1784

TENUTA'S ITALIAN RESTAURANT
2995 S Clement Ave.
414-431-1014

Visit!

BASILICA OF SAINT JOSAPHAT
2333 S Sixth St.
414-645-5623

MILWAUKEE PUBLIC MARKET
400 N Water St.
414-336-1111

NORTH POINT WATER TOWER
2288 N Lake Dr.
414-286-2830

to Do!

VILLA TERRACE DECORATIVE ARTS MUSEUM
2220 N Terrace Ave.
414-296-1101

HOLLER HOUSE
2042 W Lincoln Ave.
262-442-2517

NORTH POINT LIGHTHOUSE
2650 N Wahl Ave.
414-332-6754

HARLEY-DAVIDSON MUSEUM
400 W Canal St.
414-287-2789

FROM MILWAUKEE'S HARBOR DISTRICT, follow West Greenfield Avenue. Take a right on WI-32. Follow WI-32 through downtown to the lakefront. Continue on WI-32 North. Turn left at ALT-41/Brown Deer Road. Get on WI-57/I-43 ALT N. Turn right on North Cedarburg Road/Washington Road.

Stay!

THE IRON HORSE HOTEL
500 W Florida St.
414-374-4766

THE PFISTER HOTEL
424 E Wisconsin Ave.
414-273-8222

SHERIDAN'S BED & BREAKFAST
5133 S Lake Dr., Cudahy
414-747-9810

CEDARBURG

The Cedarburg Covered Bridge, a picturesque landmark in Ozaukee County, represents a bygone era. Built in 1876, it is one of the last remaining covered bridges in the state. Originally known as the "Red Bridge," the structure was constructed of pine with oak lattices to span Cedar Creek. Its 120-foot length and sturdy design made it a vital link for the community. Today, the bridge is closed to vehicular traffic, allowing visitors to appreciate its timeless appeal and immerse themselves in the surrounding scenery.

The tranquility of Covered Bridge Park is only one facet of Cedarburg's charm. For a deeper dive into the town's history, consider staying at one of its historic bed and breakfasts, such as the Washington House Inn or the Stagecoach Inn.

The Washington House Inn provides a charming escape in the heart of Cedarburg. Built in 1886, this historic inn exudes small-town hospitality while providing modern comforts. Its proximity to the arts and shopping make it the perfect base for exploring the area. For another historic experience, the Stagecoach Inn is a must-visit. Housed in a stone building dating to 1853, the inn maintains antique-style rooms and a glimpse into the area's past. Its quaint atmosphere and convenient location make it popular for couples and history enthusiasts. Both inns contribute to Cedarburg's allure as a destination that seamlessly blends history and modern comfort.

Eat!

THE FARMSTEAD
W62N238 Washington Ave.
262-375-2655

SAL'S PIZZA CEDARBURG
W63N635 Washington Ave.
262-375-0011

WAYNE'S DRIVE-IN
1331 Covered Bridge Rd.
262-375-9999

BOULANGERIE DU MONDE
W62N588 Washington Ave.
262-375-1050

Visit!

CEDARBURG COVERED BRIDGE
1728-1784 Covered Bridge Rd.

LION'S DEN GORGE NATURE PRESERVE
511 High Bluff Dr.
Grafton

LIME KILN PARK
2020 Green Bay Rd.
Grafton
262-375-5310

REBELLION BREWING USA
N57W6172 Portland Rd.
262-421-8678

TIP

The Pagoda Fine Jewelry shop, a distinctive pagoda-style building erected in 1926 as a Wadhams Oil and Grease Station, sits beside the historic Landmark Feed store, a former grist mill.

One of the few historic Pagoda gas stations remaining

to Do!

CEDAR CREEK WINERY
N70W6340 Bridge Rd.
262-377-8020

RIVOLI THEATRE
W62N567 Washington Ave.

WISCONSIN MUSEUM OF QUILTS & FIBER ARTS
N50W5050 Portland Rd.
262-546-0300

INTERURBAN BIKE TRAIL OZAUKEE COUNTY
W63N643 Washington Ave.

Stay!

WASHINGTON HOUSE INN
W62N573 Washington Ave.
262-375-3550

THE STAGECOACH INN BED AND BREAKFAST
W61N520 Washington Ave.
262-375-0208

GOING SOUTH FROM CEDARBURG, turn right on Portland Road. Turn left on County C. Continue straight onto County C/Lake Shore Road. Turn left onto West Chestnut Street and turn right on South Webster in Port Washington.

PORT WASHINGTON

Port Washington is home to a remarkable piece of maritime history: the 1860 Light Station. Originally constructed in 1849, the lighthouse underwent a significant reconstruction in 1860, giving it its current form. The brick tower has become a city symbol with its distinctive lantern room. The light station also housed the keeper's family, providing a glimpse into the challenging lives of those who dedicated themselves to ensuring the safety of mariners.

Today, the 1860 Light Station is a historical landmark and a museum operated by the Port Washington Historical Society. Visitors can climb the tower for breathtaking lake views and learn about the lighthouse's history. The museum exhibits offer insights into the lives of the lightkeepers and the importance of lighthouses in maritime navigation.

While the 1860 Light Station represents hope and safety for mariners, the waters off Port Washington also hold tales of tragedy. One of the most infamous shipwrecks off the coast of Port Washington is the SS *Toledo*. This passenger and freight steamer met a tragic end on October 24, 1856, when it was dashed against the rocky shoreline during a violent storm.

The wreck of the *Toledo* has become a poignant symbol of the region's maritime heritage. Today, the anchor of the *Toledo* stands as a memorial in Port Washington's Union Cemetery, a solemn reminder of the tragedy and the bravery of those involved in the rescue efforts.

Eat!

RIVERVIEW INN
3172 N Riverside Dr.
Saukville
262-284-0411

THE STEERAGE DINING SALOON
218 N Franklin St.
262-235-4281

TWISTED WILLOW RESTAURANT
308 N Franklin St.
262-268-7600

MOONLIGHT TAVERN & SUPPER CLUB
101 E Main St.
262-235-1981

FRANKIE'S ICE CREAM
(seasonal)
313 N Franklin St.

Visit!

CEDARBURG BOG STATE NATURAL AREA
WI-33, Saukville
262-675-6844

HARRINGTON BEACH STATE PARK
531 Co. Rd. D, Belgium
262-285-3015

to Do!

PORT WASHINGTON 1860 LIGHT STATION
311 Johnson St.
262-268-9150

DULUTH TRADING COMPANY
108 N Franklin St.
262-268-1305

MEMORIES BALLROOM
1077 Lake Dr.
262-284-6850

LUXEMBOURG AMERICAN CULTURAL SOCIETY & CENTER
100 Peter Thein Ave.
Belgium
262-476-5086

OZAUKEE COUNTY PIONEER VILLAGE
4880 Co. Rd. I, Saukville
262-377-4510

TIP

The Duluth Trading Company building reflects Port Washington's maritime heritage. Its rooftop proudly displays the iconic Smith Bros. Fish Shanty Restaurant sign, a nostalgic nod to the town's fishing past.

Stay!

THE HILLTOP HAVEN
W4907 Hilltop Rd.
Fredonia
920-207-7255

PORT WASHINGTON INN
308 W Washington St.
262-284-5583

THE PORT HOTEL
101 E Main St.
262-235-1990

STARTING IN PORT WASHINGTON, go north on WI-32. Turn right on County Road KW. Turn right on West Union Avenue. Go left on WI-32. Turn right on WI-28. Turn right on Pennsylvania Avenue into downtown Sheboygan.

SHEBOYGAN

The *Gallinipper*, a 95-foot wooden schooner, and Wisconsin's oldest shipwreck, stands as a haunting reminder of life on the Great Lakes. Built in 1833, the vessel was initially involved in the fur trade and later transported immigrants to Wisconsin.

On July 7, 1851, while transporting lumber, the *Gallinipper* was caught in a violent storm, capsized, and sank northeast of Sheboygan. Remarkably, all aboard were rescued.

Discovered in 1994, the shipwreck was found remarkably intact, lying upright on the lakebed. Archaeological surveys conducted by the Wisconsin Historical Society led to its placement on the National Register of Historic Places in 2010. Remains of the *Lottie Cooper,* another notable Great Lakes shipwreck, can be found in Deland Park.

Sheboygan has a blend of aquatic adventures from the depths of Lake Michigan to its shores. While the discovery of the *Gallinipper* shipwreck captivated historians, the city's beaches also hold hidden treasures for beach glass enthusiasts. The constant lapping of Lake Michigan's waves against the shoreline transforms discarded glass into smooth, translucent gems. Over time, the harsh conditions of the lake erode glass fragments, creating coveted beach glass in various colors.

Finding beach glass requires patience and a keen eye, but the rewards are undeniable. For those passionate about beachcombing, exploring the

Kohler-Andrae State Park

TIP

Housed in a restored fishing shanty, the Weather Center Café offers a charming ambiance with knotty pine walls, nautical maps, and a river view.

shoreline early in the morning or after a storm can increase the chances of finding hidden treasures. While there's no guaranteed spot for the best finds, beaches like Lake View Park and North Beach are popular for beach glass hunters.

Stay!

BLUE HARBOR RESORT
725 Blue Harbor Dr.
866- 701-2583

CASTINO LAKEVIEW MANSION
303 St. Clair Ave.
847- 877-2003

Visit!

KOHLER-ANDRAE STATE PARK
1020 Beach Park Ln.
920-451-4080

***LOTTIE COOPER* SHIPWRECK**
(in Deland Park across from Sheboygan County YMCA)
812 Broughton Dr.

Eat!

RUPP'S DOWNTOWN
925 N Eighth St.
920-459-8155

SLY'S MIDTOWN SALOON AND GRILL
508 N Eighth St.
920-783-6644

MAJERLE'S BLACK RIVER GRILL
5033 Evergreen Dr.
920-803-5115

WEATHER CENTER CAFÉ
809 Riverfront Dr.
920-459-9283

AL & AL'S STEINHAUS
1502 S 12th St.
920-452-5530

to Do!

WADE HOUSE
W7965 WI-23, Greenbush
920-526-3271

STEFANIE H. WEILL CENTER FOR THE PERFORMING ARTS
826 N Eighth St.
920-208-3243

JAMES TELLEN WOODLAND SCULPTURE GARDEN
5634 Evergreen Dr.
920-458-6144

ART PRESERVE OF THE JOHN MICHAEL KOHLER ARTS CENTER
3636 Lower Falls Rd.
920-453-0346

WAELDERHAUS
1100 W Riverside Dr.
Kohler
920-453-2851

AVIATION HERITAGE CENTER OF WISCONSIN
N6191 Resource Dr.
920-467-2043

James Tellen Woodland Sculpture Garden

HEAD NORTH from Sheboygan on WI-28. Turn right on North 15th Avenue/Lakeshore Road. Follow Lakeshore Road. Turn right on East Jefferson Avenue. Turn left on Lakeshore Drive/LS. Continue into Manitowoc.

MANITOWOC/ TWO RIVERS

Manitowoc holds a significant place in American history as a World War II Heritage City. This prestigious designation, awarded by the National Park Service, recognizes the city's crucial role in supporting the war effort.

The heart of Manitowoc's wartime contribution lies in shipbuilding. The Manitowoc Shipbuilding Company answered the nation's call by shifting its focus from commercial vessels to submarines. Led by Charles West, the company sought a contract to build destroyers for the Navy but was ultimately tasked with the more challenging submarine construction. Between 1941 and 1945, the company produced an impressive 28 submarines for the US Navy, earning the coveted Minuteman "Bullseye" banner for 100 percent worker participation in war bond sales.

Beyond shipbuilding, Manitowoc's industries contributed to the war effort in various ways. Aluminum Goods Manufacturing, Burger Boat, Lakeside

Packaging, and Heresite Protective Coatings played vital roles in producing essential war materials. These companies manufactured everything from oil tanks for B-29 bombers to critical items such as meal cans and torpedo coatings.

Today, Manitowoc honors its WWII legacy through various initiatives, including the Wisconsin Maritime Museum, which houses the USS Cobia submarine. The John D. Dingell Jr. Conservation, Management, and Recreation Act of 2019 stipulates that only one city, township, or municipality per state can be designated as a World War II Heritage City. This honorable designation solidifies Manitowoc's place in American history and ensures that the sacrifices and contributions of its citizens are never forgotten.

TIP

SubFest is a four-day celebration of Manitowoc's submarine heritage. This family-friendly event features the USS *Cobia*, hands-on activities, live music, and delicious food.

Eat!

BUD WILLMAN'S LUNCH
1901 Washington St.
Manitowoc
920-684-0005

WAVERLY INN PUB & PIZZERIA
1402 16th St., Two Rivers
920-794-1709

COURTHOUSE PUB
1001 S Eighth St.
Manitowoc
920-686-1166

CONNIE'S DINER
1303 22nd St.
Two Rivers
920-794-8500

Stay!

TOLL HOUSE BED & BREAKFAST
2004 Menasha Ave.
Manitowoc
920-323-7976

DEVILS RIVER CAMPGROUND (ROCK MILL HISTORICAL SITE)
16612 Co. Rd. R, Maribel
920-863-2812

Visit!

POINT BEACH STATE FOREST AND RAWLEY POINT LIGHTHOUSE
9400 Co. Rd. O
Two Rivers
920-794-7480

CHERNEY MARIBEL CAVES COUNTY PARK
15401 Co. Rd. R
Maribel
920-683-4185

STILL BEND/SCHWARTZ HOUSE
3425 Adams St.
Two Rivers
612- 840-7507

to Do!

WISCONSIN MARITIME MUSEUM
75 Maritime Dr.
Manitowoc
920-684-0218

ROGERS STREET FISHING VILLAGE
2102 Jackson St.
Two Rivers
920-793-5905

RAHR-WEST ART MUSEUM
610 N Eighth St.
Manitowoc
920-686-3090

BEERNTSEN'S CONFECTIONARY
108 N Eighth St.
Manitowoc
920-684-9616

HAMILTON WOOD TYPE & PRINTING MUSEUM
1816 10th St., Two Rivers
920-794-6272

ARIENS CO. MUSEUM
109 Calumet St., Brillion
920-756-4455

FROM MANITOWOC, take WI-42 N. Turn right on Lake Street and continue to Algoma's lakefront.

ALGOMA

The discovery of the *Margaret A. Muir* in May 2024 sent ripples through the maritime history community. Built in Manitowoc in 1872, the 130-foot, three-masted schooner vanished following a catastrophic storm on September 30, 1893.

Carrying a cargo of salt from Bay City, Michigan, to South Chicago, Illinois, the *Muir* encountered a violent storm that proved too formidable. The crew, including Captain David Clow, managed to escape in a lifeboat, but the ship and its cargo were lost to the depths of Lake Michigan.

The wreck's remarkable preservation, found in just 50 feet of water off the coast of Algoma, provides an unprecedented opportunity to study 19th-century shipbuilding and maritime life. Archaeologists and historians are eager to explore the vessel's remains, hoping to uncover clues about its construction, its cargo, and the lives of its crew.

The discovery of the *Muir* has ignited a passion for underwater exploration. To experience maritime history up close, visit the *Tug Ludington*, docked in

Look for murals throughout Algoma.

Lake Michigan view from the Crescent Beach Boardwalk

Kewaunee at Harbor Park. This 115-foot seagoing tug, built in 1943, played a vital role in World War II, participating in the D-Day invasion by towing ammunition barges across the English Channel.

After the war, the tug continued to serve, assisting in harbor construction and maintenance on the Great Lakes. Eventually, it found its permanent home in Kewaunee. Visitors can step aboard this historic vessel and explore its inner workings, gaining a firsthand appreciation for the conditions faced by its crew.

TIP

For a free and fun family activity, immerse yourself in Algoma's rich history with the vibrant Walldog murals, which offer a colorful snapshot of the town's past and present.

Eat!

SON OF SKALIWAGS
312 Clark St.
920-536-1539

CAFFÉ TLAZO
607 Fourth St.
920-487-7240

THREE ELEVEN BAR & BISTRO
311 Steele St.
920-487-8065

NORTH WATER BAKERY & DELI
133 Water St.
920-487-5306

VILLAGE KITCHEN
101 Old Orchard Ave., Casco
920-837-7333

Visit!

ALGOMA PIERHEAD LIGHTHOUSE
1 Steele St.
Tug Ludington
213 Harrison St., Kewaunee
920-388-5000

KEWAUNEE PIERHEAD LIGHTHOUSE
Ellis St., Kewaunee

WORLD'S TALLEST GRANDFATHER CLOCK
322 Milwaukee St., Kewaunee

Stay!

HOTEL STEBBINS
201 Steele St.
920-487-5521

KEWAUNEE RV & CAMPGROUND
333 Terraqua Dr., Kewaunee
920-388-4851

to Do!

VON STIEHL WINERY
115 Navarino St.
920-487-5208

CRESCENT BEACH BOARDWALK
1025 Lake St.
920-487-2041

HARBOR POINT PARK
110 Hathaway Dr., Kewaunee

OLD FIREHOUSE MUSEUM
Milwaukee St. and Miller St.
Kewaunee
920-255-1139

Von Stiehl Winery is within walking distance of Lake Michigan's shoreline.

LAKE SUPERIOR
DULUTH
SUPERIOR
WASHBURN
APOSTLE ISLANDS
ASHLAND
IRONWOOD
CHEQUAMEGON NATIONAL FOREST
LAND O' LAKES
DANBURY
HAYWARD
PARK FALLS
EAGLE RIVER
NICOLET NATIONAL FOREST
SPOONER
KINSFORD
PHILLIPS
RHINELANDER
CAMERON
LADYSMITH
MERRILL
MEDFORD
ANTIGO
WISCONSIN
CHIPPEWA FALLS
WAUSAU
OCONTO FALLS
MENOMONIE
EAU CLAIRE
MARSHFIELD
SHAWANO
CLINTONVILLE
MONDOVI
NEILLSVILLE
STEVENS POINT
WISCONSIN RAPIDS
WHITEHALL
WAUPACA
APPLETON
BLACK RIVER FALLS
PETENWELL DAM
MISSISSIPPI RIVER
WAUTOMA
TOMAH
CASTLE ROCK LAKE
OSHKOSH
LAKE WINNEBAGO
LA CROSSE
NEW LISBON
WESTBY
PORTAGE
BEAVER DAM
WEST BEND
RICHLAND CENTER
IOWA
BOSCOBEL
LAKE MENDOTA
MADISON
DODGEVILLE
STOUGHTON
LANCASTER
JANESVILLE
MONROE
DUBUQUE

CENTRAL WISCONSIN:

CRANBERRIES AND CHEESE

From the Cranberry Highway and a distinguished natural landmark to a former Wisconsin World's Fair pavilion and a round barn hailed as the largest in the world, Central Wisconsin delivers an unforgettable road trip ending with a beverage from a Civil War–era brewery.

Located near Wausau, Rib Mountain is the prominent geological feature of the landscape. Visitors can hike to the summit via trails or ride by car up Rib Mountain Drive to take in its spectacular views.

Marshfield is home to an iconic Round Barn. This distinctive 1898 structure was a popular design in the late 19th century and today is proclaimed the "World's Largest Round Barn."

The small town of Neillsville features the 1964 Wisconsin World's Fair Pavilion. This innovative structure was built for the New York World's Fair and later relocated to Neillsville. The pavilion showcases 1964 World's Fair exhibits and has a nice gift shop with Wisconsin-made ice cream and locally made cheese.

Sightseeing on the Cranberry Highway provides a scenic journey through Wisconsin's cranberry-growing region, spanning approximately 50 miles from Wisconsin Rapids to Warrens and between Pittsville and Nekoosa. This self-guided drive presents an opportunity to explore the heart of the state's cranberry industry.

An excellent place to finish the route is in Stevens Point. Point Brewery's history goes back to the Civil War era, when German immigrants established the brewery. Over the years, the brewery has faced challenges, including Prohibition. Today, visitors can tour the historic brewery and learn about the brewing process.

TO START THE TOUR, BEGIN IN DOWNTOWN WAUSAU at the Grand Theater and continue the drive which ends in Stevens Point.

Downtown Wausau
Courtesy of Tim Manus

WAUSAU

While Wausau is renowned for its lumbering past, another significant chapter in its history involves ginseng cultivation. This delicate root, prized in traditional Chinese medicine, thrived in the region's rich soil and climate.

The late 19th century marked the beginning of ginseng cultivation in Wausau. Local farmers, recognizing the plant's economic potential, began experimenting with growing ginseng on their land. John Koehler, a prominent figure in the industry, played a pivotal role in establishing Wausau as a ginseng hub. He successfully cultivated ginseng on a larger scale and formed the Wausau Ginseng Company in 1908.

Wausau's fertile soil and favorable climate created ideal conditions for ginseng growth. Ginseng cultivation became a cornerstone of the local agricultural landscape. International markets sought after the high-quality roots produced here. At its peak, Wausau was a major worldwide exporter of ginseng, contributing significantly to the local economy.

Today, while the industry has evolved, ginseng remains an integral part of Wausau's heritage. Wisconsin is the leading ginseng producer in the United States, producing over one million pounds of ginseng, which accounts for 98 percent of US ginseng production and 10 percent of the world's supply. Each year, Wausau hosts the International Wisconsin Ginseng Festival, which celebrates the region's rich history surrounding this uncommon crop.

Eat!

PALMS SUPPER CLUB
5912 Business Hwy. 51 S
Schofield
715-359-2200

KREGER'S BAKERY
1506 N Third St.
715-845-3644

SAM'S PIZZA
111 Elm St. #4669
715-842-3165

TIMEKEEPER DISTILLERY
720 Grant St.
715-679-3777

ANGELO'S FAMILY PIZZERIA
1206 N Sixth St.
715-845-6225

Visit!

GRAND THEATER
401 N Fourth St.
715-842-0988

MONK BOTANICAL GARDENS
1800 N First Ave.
715-261-6309

45 X 90 GEOGRAPHICAL MARKER
5651 Meridian Rd.
Athens
715-261-1550

RIB MOUNTAIN STATE PARK & OBSERVATION TOWER
149801 State Park Rd.
715-842-2522

Stay!

STEWART INN
521 Grant St.
262-639-5500

JEFFERSON STREET INN
201 Jefferson St.
715-907-8975

INN AT THE RIVER
2625 Northwestern Ave.
715-449-2091

3RD ST. LOFTS
615 N Third St.
715-323-2010

to Do!

LEIGH YAWKEY WOODSON ART MUSEUM
700 N 12th St.
715-845-7010

WAUSAU WHITEWATER PARK
200 River Dr.
715-203-1279

TIP

Hsu's Ginseng Enterprises, Inc., the largest ginseng farming operation in the US, offers tours of its operations, from seed to root harvest, including a stop at the cultivating gardens.

TAKE US-51 S FROM WAUSAU. Take exit 188 and County Road N. Turn left onto WI-107 S. Turn right onto WI-153 W. Turn left onto South Third Avenue. Turn left onto WI-97 S.

MARSHFIELD

Marshfield has transformed from a small settlement to a regional powerhouse, carving a distinctive niche through health care innovation and agricultural ingenuity. This remarkable journey is a source of pride for the city's residents and an example of their hard work and dedication.

Initially a lumbering town, Marshfield's economy diversified over time. Recognizing the region's fertile lands, residents turned to agriculture, particularly dairy farming. This transition laid the foundation for Marshfield's role as a significant contributor to Wisconsin's dairy industry.

World's Largest Round Barn
Courtesy of Tim Manus

Marshfield's agricultural heritage is showcased by the iconic Round Barn. This colossal structure, erected in 1916, once housed livestock and is often hailed as the world's largest round barn. This architectural marvel is an example of the ingenuity and scale of early 20th–century farming practices. Today, it remains a captivating sight, drawing visitors from far and wide.

The city's most enduring legacy, however, lies in health care. The Marshfield Clinic, founded in 1915, has evolved from a small group practice into a renowned health care system. Its commitment to patient-centered care, medical research, and community outreach has positioned Marshfield as a leader in the field. The clinic's impact extends far beyond the city limits, drawing patients from across the region and beyond.

Today, Marshfield is a thriving community that dedicates itself to health care and agriculture and takes great pride in preserving its symbolic landmarks.

Eat!

BELVEDERE SUPPER CLUB
203630 WI-97
715-387-4161

MELODY GARDENS
1200 S Oak Ave.
715-384-3326

THE HIDEOUT
10150 US-10
715-676-2226

NUTZ DEEP II
809 S Central Ave.
715-387-2597

BLUE HERON BREWPUB
108 W Ninth St.
715-389-1868

TIP

Stop by Weber's Farm Store in Marshfield for a delicious ice cream cone. My favorite is a vanilla soft serve cone dipped in sprinkles.

Visit!

WORLD'S LARGEST ROUND BARN
513 E 17th St.
715-387-1261

THIMBLEBERRY BOOKS
166 S Central Ave.
715-387-3049

SOO LINE STEAM LOCOMOTIVE 2442
1800 S Roddis Ave.

JURUSTIC PARK
112021 Old Sugarbush Ln.
715-387-1653

SENIOR CRAFT SHOPPE
450 S Central Ave.
715-384-2230

to Do!

WEBER'S FARM STORE
9706 Co. Rd. H
715-384-5639

NASONVILLE DAIRY STORE
10898 US-10
715-676-2177

WILDWOOD ZOO
608 W 17th St.
715-486-2056

MARSHFIELD CURLING CLUB
1500 S Vine Ave.
715-384-9425

FROM MARSHFIELD, follow WI-13 BUS S. At the traffic circle, take the first exit onto WI-13 BUS S. At the traffic circle, take the second exit onto US-10 W. Follow US-10 W into Neillsville.

NEILLSVILLE

Neillsville's claim to fame lies in its possession of a remarkable structure: the Wisconsin Pavilion from the 1964 New York World's Fair. The Wisconsin Pavilion was a standout attraction. It was designed to showcase the best of the Badger State. Its most notable feature was a colossal block of cheese, a symbol of the state's rich dairy heritage.

Beyond the cheese, the pavilion offered a glimpse into the state's astonishing landscape, showcasing its forests, lakes, and outdoor recreation opportunities. Interactive exhibits brought the wonders of Wisconsin to life, engaging visitors of all ages. Incorporating elements of the state's Native American heritage added a unique touch. With its emphasis on food, nature, and culture, the Wisconsin Pavilion successfully captured the essence of the Badger State, leaving a lasting impression on millions of fairgoers.

After the fair, the fate of this iconic building was uncertain, with demolition looming. Howie Sturtz and Wayne Grap, owners of Central Wisconsin Broadcasting, had a vision that saved the building. They purchased the pavilion and transported it to Neillsville, preserving a piece of history. The journey to bring this architectural marvel to its new home was challenging. It required meticulous planning and execution. But once in place, the pavilion was transformed into a radio station, breathing new life into the historic structure and giving it a permanent location on US Highway 10.

Visit!

REED SCHOOL
4326 US-10
715-743-2239

PAVILION CHEESE & GIFTS
1201 E Division St.
715-743-3333

CHATTY BELLE
1200 E Division St.

LISTEMAN ARBORETUM
W Division St.
715-743-2105

UNITED STATES POST OFFICE
619 Hewett St.
715-743-2842

to Do!

THE HIGHGROUND VETERANS MEMORIAL PARK
W7031 W Ridge Rd.
715-743-4224

SILVER DOME BALLROOM
W7670 US-10
612- 803-7362

THORP AREA HISTORICAL MUSEUM
307 W Birch St., Thorp
715-669-5943

BRANSTITER MUSEUM
600 S Main St., Greenwood
715-267-6205

LA GRANDER'S HILLSIDE DAIRY
W11299 Broek Rd., Stanley
715-644-2275

1897 CLARK COUNTY JAIL MUSEUM
215 E Fifth St.
715-743-2150

Eat!

FANNIES SUPPER CLUB & MOTEL
W3741 US-10
715-743-2169

THE ROOTBEER STAND
101 W Mill St., Loyal
715-503-1004

Stay!

TUFTS' MANSION BED & BREAKFAST
26 Hewett St.
715-743-3346

WEDGES CREEK HIDEAWAY
W7355 Mann Rd., Greenwood
715-386-5466

LEAVING NEILLSVILLE, take WI-73 S. Right on County Highway B. Right onto County Highway EX. Left onto WI-54 E. Right onto WI-54 E/State Rd, 80 S. Left onto WI-54 E. Left onto Port Rd. Right on Seneca Road. Left on WI-73. Right onto WI-13.

TIP

Inside the Neillsville Post Office is a mural titled *The Choosing of the County Seat*, painted in 1940 as part of the Great Depression New Deal.

Have a chat with the World's Largest Talking Cow. Courtesy of Tim Manus

WISCONSIN RAPIDS

TIP

Cranberry harvest season typically occurs in September and October. To confirm tour availability and schedules, check the websites or contact the farms directly.

Wisconsin Rapids, a city along the winding Wisconsin River, has a robust relationship with the state's natural resources. Once a bustling lumber town, the city transformed its economy to focus on agriculture, particularly dairy farming. However, the vibrant red hue of cranberries has truly put Wisconsin Rapids on the map.

Extending for approximately 50 miles from Wisconsin Rapids to Warrens, the Cranberry Highway winds through the heart of Cranberry Country. As a picturesque route, the highway allows a chance to explore the history and process of cranberry cultivation and witness the vast cranberry marshes, particularly during the enchanting harvest season.

Many cranberry farms offer tours, allowing visitors to better appreciate this iconic Wisconsin crop. The thrilling experience of witnessing the harvest, when the marshes are flooded and the bright red berries float to the surface, is a rare and exciting opportunity. Coupled with the chance to sample delicious cranberry products, the Cranberry Highway presents an unforgettable adventure.

The Cranberry Highway also showcases the natural beauty of Wisconsin. Lush forests, sparkling lakes, and charming small towns dot the landscape. Whether you're a nature enthusiast, a foodie craving cranberry-infused treats, or simply seeking a scenic drive, the Cranberry Highway delivers a diverse range of experiences.

Stay!

LECHATEAU THE MANOR B&B
840 First St. N
608-572-0985

THE WHITE HOUSE OF WISCONSIN RAPIDS
820 First St. N
715-248-0486

Eat!

DAIRY TREAT
1110 W Grand Ave.

LAKE AIRE SUPPER CLUB
6510 State Hwy. 13 S.
715-325-5147

CRANBERRY COUNTRY CAFÉ
204 Main St., Warrens
608-378-4878

Visit!

GEOGRAPHICAL CENTER OF THE STATE OF WISCONSIN
8335 Veedum St.
Pittsville

STATE HISTORIC MARKER #86 CRANBERRY CULTURE
North Side of State Hwy. 54

WISCONSIN FIRE & EMS MEMORIAL
Ben Hanson Park
2031 Second Ave. S
715-302-0100

NECEDAH NATIONAL WILDLIFE REFUGE VISITOR CENTER
N11385 Headquarters Rd., Necedah
608-565-2551

RUDOLPH GROTTO GARDENS
6975 Grotto Ave.
Rudolph
715-435-3120

SANDHILL STATE WILDLIFE AREA
1715 Co. Hwy. X
Babcock
715-884-2437

to Do!

SPLASH OF RED CRANBERRY TOURS
5407 First Ave., Pittsville
715-884-6412

DISCOVER CRANBERRIES MUSEUM
204 Main St., Warrens
608-378-4878

WISCONSIN DAIRY STATE CHEESE COMPANY
6860 WI-34, Rudolph
715-435-3144

WETHERBY CRANBERRY FARM
3365 Auger Rd., Warrens
608-378-4813

FROM WISCONSIN RAPIDS, take WI-13 N. Turn right onto WI-66 E. Continue on WI-66 into Stevens Point.

STEVENS POINT

Stevens Point Brewery is a cornerstone of Wisconsin's brewing heritage. Founded in 1857, it's one of the oldest continuously operating breweries in the United States. The brewery has weathered countless storms, from Prohibition to changing consumer tastes, yet it has managed to maintain its place as a Wisconsin institution.

Over the years, Stevens Point Brewery has produced a variety of beers, many of which have become local favorites. Its commitment to quality and consistency has earned it a loyal following. The brewery has also been instrumental in revitalizing the craft beer scene in Wisconsin, introducing innovative brews while staying true to its classic recipes.

Today, Stevens Point Brewery remains a vital part of the community, drawing visitors who experience its history and taste its beers. The brewery offers tours, tastings, and a lively taproom, providing a glimpse into the world of craft brewing.

The *Boy with the Leaking Boot*

Another noteworthy symbol of Stevens Point is the "Boy with the Leaking Boot" statue. Originally a drinking fountain, it was erected in 1895 and has become a beloved local landmark. The sculpture depicts a young boy holding a boot with water pouring out. Over the years, the statue has endured its share of challenges. It has been vandalized, moved, and restored multiple times. Despite these setbacks, the community's affection for the boy has remained steadfast, making him a quirky and cherished part of Stevens Point.

Eat!

THE WOODEN CHAIR
1059 Main St.
715-341-1133

BILL'S PIZZA SHOP
1101 Main St.
715-344-9557

SILVER COACH
38 Park Ridge Dr.
715-341-6588

Visit!

THE BOY WITH THE LEAKY BOOT
Stevens Point Fire Department
1701 Franklin St.
715-344-1833

STEVENS POINT BREWERY
2617 Water St.
715-344-9310

THE MAIN GRAIN BAKERY
1009 First St., Suite C
715-630-1486

BLOCHER PLANETARIUM
University of Wisconsin–Stevens Point
2001 Fourth Ave.
715-346-2120

STEVENS POINT SCULPTURE PARK
901 Second St. N

Stay!

DREAMS OF YESTERYEAR BED & BREAKFAST
1100 Brawley St.
715-341-4525

THE INN AT SENTRYWORLD
501 Michigan Ave. N
715-345-1600

to Do!

SCHMEECKLE RESERVE AND GREEN CIRCLE TRAIL
2419 N Point Dr.
715-346-4992

HISTORIC FIREHOUSE NO.2
1949 Strongs Ave.
715-600-4930

RIVERFRONT ARTS CENTER
1200 Crosby Ave.
715-343-6251

GEPETTO'S WORKSHOP
1121 Main St.
715-341-8640

TIP

The *Boy with the Leaking Boot* statue is displayed outdoors only from Memorial Day to Labor Day. Otherwise, he finds safety in the basement of the fire department.

MINNESOTA
LAKE SUPERIOR
DULUTH
SUPERIOR
BAYFIELD
APOSTLE ISLANDS
WASHBURN
ASHLAND
IRONWOOD
CHEQUAMEGON NATIONAL FOREST
LAND O' LAKES
DANBURY
HAYWARD
SPOONER
SIREN
PARK FALLS
EAGLE RIVER
NICOLET NATIONAL FOREST
PHILLIPS
RICE LAKE
RHINELANDER
ST. CROIX FALLS
CAMERON
LADYSMITH
MERRILL
NEW RICHMOND
MEDFORD
ANTIGO
NNEAPOLIS
ST PAUL
WISCONSIN
CHIPPEWA FALLS
MENOMONIE
PRESCOTT
EAU CLAIRE
MARSHFIELD
MONDOVI
NEILLSVILLE
STEVENS POINT
WHITEHALL
WISCONSIN RAPIDS
WAUPACA
BLACK RIVER FALLS
PETENWELL DAM
MISSISSIPPI RIVER
WAUTOMA
TOMAH
CASTLE ROCK LAKE
LA CROSSE
NEW LISBON
WESTBY
PORTAGE
RICHLAND CENTER
IOWA
BOSCOBEL
LAKE MENDOTA
MADISON
DODGEVILLE
STOUGHTON
LANCASTER
MONROE
DUBUQUE
ILLINOIS

NORTHWEST:

NATIONAL FORESTS, RIVERS, AND LAKES

Northwest Wisconsin, renowned for its natural beauty, offers a diverse range of outdoor adventures and cultural experiences. From the towering pines of the Chequamegon-Nicolet National Forest to the pristine waters of Lake Superior, this region is a paradise for scenic road trips and history buffs alike.

Northwest Wisconsin's history is rooted in its lumbering past. Visit the Lumberjack World Championships in Hayward to learn about the region's logging heritage. Or explore the Gandy Dancer Trail, a former railroad corridor transformed into a recreational trail.

Take a scenic break by discovering hidden waterfalls and viewing the St. Croix River, a designated National Scenic Riverway. Visit the Fresh Water Fishing Hall of Fame, home to the iconic giant 143-foot-long muskie statue. Climb inside, then scan the Northwoods' horizon from inside its mouth. Farther north, the Apostle Islands National Lakeshore, a group of 22 islands in Lake Superior, offers stunning scenery and opportunities for kayaking, camping, and exploring sea caves.

The Wisconsin Great Northern Railroad provides a nostalgic journey through the Northwoods, while the Osceola & St. Croix Valley Railway provides picturesque views of the St. Croix River. Scenic cruises also offer a leisurely way to enjoy the region's natural beauty. Take a boat tour on Lake Superior to admire the Apostle Islands or explore the St. Croix River and its historic towns.

From the rugged beauty of its forests and lakes to its rich cultural heritage, Northwest Wisconsin is an ideal destination for history buffs and road warriors seeking scenic adventures.

TO START THE TOUR, BEGIN IN DOWNTOWN SPOONER on Walnut Street. The drive will make a loop ending in Rice Lake.

SPOONER

The Wisconsin Great Northern Railroad allows a unique opportunity to step back in time and experience the magic of rail travel. This historic line, winding through the heart of Wisconsin's Northwoods, invites passengers on a nostalgic journey that combines comfort, history, and beautiful scenery.

Passengers can choose from various experiences in train cars which have been painstakingly restored, each with an out-of-the-ordinary perspective. The Bed & Breakfast train is a highlight, offering passengers luxury reminiscent of the golden age of rail travel. Popular rides include the Family Pizza Train, the Wine and Cheese Train, and the Scenic Sightseeing Ride. As the train glides along the tracks, passengers are treated to the natural scenery of farmland, dense forests, and the scenic Namekagon River.

Exchange the serene train ride for the energy of the Stone Lake Cranberry Festival. The small town of Stone Lake transforms into a hub of cranberry-themed festivities with its annual celebration. Held on the first Saturday of October, the event celebrates the region's cranberry heritage and draws more than 30,000 visitors.

At the center of the event are arts and crafts showcasing the work of local artisans and cranberry marsh tours. Food enthusiasts can indulge in cranberry-infused treats, from sweet to savory, and even purchase fresh cranberries directly from local farmers. Children are entertained with face painting, games, and race in the ever-popular Krate Derby, a unique and exciting race featuring homemade wooden cars.

TIP

On the Bed & Breakfast Train, enjoy a cocktail on a restored 1951 Montana Ranch Train Car, one of six lounge cars built for the Great Northern Railway's Empire Builder line.

The Potter's Shed Gallery

Stay!

COBBLESTONE BED AND BREAKFAST
319 S Main St., Birchwood
715-354-3494

HUNT HILL AUDUBON SANCTUARY CABINS
N2384 Hunt Hill Rd.
Sarona, 715-635-6543

THE BOXCAR (AIRBNB)
W7207 Cable Lake Rd.

Eat!

ROUND MAN BREWING CO.
234 Walnut St.
715-939-1800

MARY'S BLUEGILL BAR & GRILL
109 S Main St., Birchwood
715-354-7949

PINE RIDGE
16618W N Sissabagama Rd., Stone Lake
715-865-2796

LAKEVIEW BAR AND GRILL
5 W Fifth Ave., Shell Lake
715-731-0080

THE DOCK COFFEE
218 Walnut St.
715-635-1919

Visit!

HUNT HILL AUDUBON SANCTUARY AND DORY'S BOG
N2384 Hunt Hill Rd.
Sarona
715-635-6543

ST. CROIX NATIONAL SCENIC RIVERWAYS VISITOR CENTER
W5483 US Hwy. 63
Trego
715-635-8346

to Do!

WISCONSIN GREAT NORTHERN RAILROAD
N6639 Dilly Lake Rd.
Trego
715-635-3200

RAILROAD MEMORIES MUSEUM
424 N Front St.
715-635-3325

WISCONSIN CANOE HERITAGE MUSEUM
312 N Front St.
715-635-5002

RED SCHOOLHOUSE WINES
5768 N Fourth St. S
Stone Lake
715-865-5038

THE POTTER'S SHED GALLERY
260 Industrial Blvd.
Shell Lake
715-468-4122

FROM SPOONER, head southeast on WI-70 E. Turn left onto WI-27 N into Hayward.

HAYWARD

Hayward's roots are deeply intertwined with the lumber industry. Founded in the 1880s, the town grew rapidly as a center for logging and timber processing. While the lumber era has passed, the town's identity is rooted in its lumberjack heritage, and no experience captures the spirit of the Northwoods better than Scheer's Lumberjack Shows. This thrilling spectacle showcases the athleticism and skill of world-class lumberjacks, offering a glimpse into a bygone era.

The show occurs in the Lumberjack Bowl, the same arena hosting the renowned Lumberjack World Championships. Spectators are treated to a high-energy performance featuring a variety of competitions, including log rolling, pole climbing, axe throwing, and the thrilling hot saw event.

Hayward is also synonymous with fishing, and no symbol better represents this aquatic passion than the colossal fiberglass muskie that dominates the skyline. This larger-than-life sculpture, a hallmark of the National Fresh Water Fishing Hall of Fame, is a must-see.

At 143 feet long and four and a half stories tall, this gigantic creature is a nod to the legendary status of the muskie, a prized catch for anglers worldwide. The sculpture is more than just a roadside attraction; it's an interactive experience. Visitors can climb inside the muskie's tooth-filled gaping jaw for a panoramic view of town.

Surrounding the muskie is a "sea of fishes," featuring monumental replicas of other popular freshwater species. This collection, combined with the museum's extensive exhibits, creates a captivating underwater world for visitors of all ages.

TIP

Backroads Coffee once housed a blacksmith shop in Hayward's early days. Its preserved brickwork, wooden beams, and arched windows offer a glimpse into the past.

Visit!

MOCCASIN BAR
15820 US-63
715-634-4211

LAKE HELANE STATE NATURAL AREA
13354 Lake Helane Rd.
608-266-0394

Take a walk into the mouth of the Musky at The Freshwater Fishing Hall of Fame.

to Do!

SCHEER'S LUMBERJACK SHOW
15640 Co. Rd. B
715-634-6923

FRESHWATER FISHING HALL OF FAME
10360 Hall of Fame Dr.
715-634-4440

ANGRY MINNOW BREWERY
10440 Florida Ave.
715-934-3055

TREMBLAY'S SWEET SHOP
10569 Main St.
715-634-2785

SAMUEL C. JOHNSON FAMILY OUTDOOR CENTER
12205 W Co. Hwy. OO
970- 634-5025

Eat!

SAWMILL SALOON
13505 US-63
715-634-5660

COOP'S PIZZA
10588 California Ave.
715-634-3027

BACKROADS COFFEE
10526 Dakota Ave.
715-634-4950

ANGLER'S BAR AND GRILL
10547 Main St.
715-634-4700

Stay!

SPIDER LAKE LODGE BED AND BREAKFAST
10472 Murphy Blvd.
715-462-3793

ANGLER'S HAVEN RESORT
15437 N Hwy. KK
715-634-2757

MCCORMICK HOUSE INN
10634 Kansas Ave.
715-934-3339

NORTHWOODS MOTEL
9854N WI-27
715-634-8088

TAKE US-63 N FROM HAYWARD. Turn right on US-2 E. Keep right through the traffic circle. Follow US-2 into Ashland.

ASHLAND

Ashland has transformed its cityscape into a vibrant outdoor gallery through its impressive collection of public murals. This initiative, spearheaded by local artists Kelly Meredith and Susan Prentice Martinsen, has earned Ashland the title "Historic Mural Capital of Wisconsin."

Over 20 large-scale murals adorn the buildings of Ashland's historic Main Street district. These colorful artworks showcase the city's rich history, from its lumberjack days to its maritime heritage. Viewers can witness the evolution of Ashland through the eyes of its artists.

One of the most notable murals celebrates the city's railroad history, paying homage to the men and women who built and operated the railroads that connected the region.

Another artwork pays tribute to the city's iconic ore dock. On the side of a Main Street building, this sprawling wall painting depicts the dock's

Aerial view of Downtown Ashland Courtesy of Tim Manus

significance in Ashland's identity. The mural is a meticulously detailed representation of the 1,800-foot-long concrete structure, accurately capturing its imposing scale and intricate design. The upper portion of the mural offers a bird's-eye view of the dock, showcasing its numerous ore chutes in precise detail. Below the aerial view, a series of "postcards" unfolds, narrating the dock's rich history.

TIP

Book Across the Bay is a winter festival transforming frozen Lake Superior into a skiing and snowshoeing wonderland. The 10-kilometer course is illuminated by candles, creating a truly enchanting atmosphere.

Each of the 23 historic murals tells a unique story, reflecting the diverse character of Ashland. The city's murals have become a source of pride for residents and a popular attraction for visitors. Whether you're an art enthusiast or simply looking for a unique way to explore the city, a mural walk is an unforgettable experience.

Eat!

GOOD THYME RESTAURANT AND CATERING
77180 State Hwy. 13
Washburn
715-373-5255

DELTA DINER
14385 Co. Hwy. H
Mason
715-372-6666

DEEP WATER GRILLE
808 Main St. W
715-682-4200

Stay!

THE INN AT TIMBER COVE
1319 Sanborn Ave.
715-682-9600

MISSION SPRINGS RESORT
30175 Mission Springs Rd.
715-209-8321

DELTA LODGE & CABINS RESORT
13565 Scenic Dr.
Iron River
715-372-4299

RIVER ROCK INN
1200 Lake Shore Dr.
715-682-3232

BEST WESTERN THE HOTEL CHEQUAMEGON
101 Lake Shore Dr. W
715-682-9095

Ashland's Big Bass Courtesy of Tim Manus

to Do!

COPPER FALLS STATE PARK
36764 Copper Falls Rd.
Mellen
715-274-5123

BAY THEATER
420 Main St. W
715-682-3555

POTATO RIVER FALLS
Potato River Falls Rd.
Saxon

OULU GLASS GALLERY
1695 W Colby Rd., Brule
715-372-4160

ST. PETER'S DOME NATIONAL NATURAL AREA
Forest Rd. 199
Marengo
888-936-7463

Visit!

NORTHERN GREAT LAKES VISITOR CENTER
29270 Co. Hwy. G
715-685-9983

HEAD SOUTHWEST ON US-2 W. Keep right to continue toward WI-13 N. Turn right onto WI-13. Turn right on Rittenhouse Avenue. Turn right on South Third Street in Bayfield.

BAYFIELD

Gateway to the Apostle Islands National Lakeshore
Courtesy of Tim Manus

Madeline Island, a 20-minute ferry ride from Bayfield and the largest of the Apostle Islands, is where the echoes of the past resonate with the beauty of the present. Long before European settlers arrived, the island was a sacred and vital place for the Ojibwe people, whose legacy continues to shape the island's identity.

For centuries, the Ojibwe, or Chippewa, people called Madeline Island home. The island served as a spiritual and cultural center, where they held ceremonies, shared stories, and maintained their traditions.

Madeline Island, known as *Mooningwanekaaning* ("The Home of the Golden Breasted Woodpecker") in the Ojibwe language, was a central gathering place for the Anishinaabe people. They believed that the Great Spirit, Gitche Manitou, had instructed them to travel west to this land of abundance.

The arrival of European fur traders in the 17th century marked a turning point in the island's history. French explorers, such as Etienne Brulé, established trading posts, initiating a period of cultural exchange and adaptation. The Ojibwe and French coexisted, forming complex relationships that shaped the island's future.

Today, the legacy of the Ojibwe people is still evident. The Madeline Island Museum celebrates the history and culture of the island's original inhabitants. While few Ojibwe people reside on the island, their spiritual connection to the land remains strong.

The island's current name is a tribute to Madeleine Cadotte, daughter of Chief White Crane and wife of a French fur trader. It symbolizes the intertwined histories of the Ojibwe and European cultures.

Stay!

PINEHURST INN BED & BREAKFAST
83645 State Hwy. 13
715-779-3676

QUEEN'S VIEW BAYFIELD
108 N Third St.
715-600-1260

LE CHATEAU BOUTIN
7 Rice Ave.
715-779-5111

OLD RITTENHOUSE INN
301 Rittenhouse Ave.
715-779-5111

Eat!

GREUNKE'S FIRST STREET INN & DINING
17 Rittenhouse Ave.
715-779-5480

MANYPENNY BISTRO
201 Manypenny Ave.
715-913-0303

PIER PLAZA RESTAURANT
1 Rittenhouse Ave.
715-779-3330

TIP

For an in-depth guided fishing experience in the Apostle Islands, cast a line with Reel Island Adventures and its expert guide, a Wisconsin DNR fisheries specialist.

to Do!

APOSTLE ISLANDS NATIONAL LAKESHORE—HEADQUARTERS
415 Washington Ave.
715-779-3397

APOSTLE ISLANDS CRUISES
2 Front St.
715-779-3925

MADELINE ISLAND MUSEUM
226 Colonel Woods Ave.
La Pointe
715-747-2415

BIG TOP CHAUTAUQUA
32525 Ski Hill Rd.
715-373-5552

REEL ISLAND ADVENTURES—APOSTLE ISLANDS CHARTERED FISHING
37600 Onigamiing Dr.
440-228-5670

ECKELS POTTERY AND FINE CRAFT GALLERY
85205 State Hwy. 13
715-779-5617

Visit!

FROG BAY TRIBAL NATIONAL PARK
92060-92070 Frog Bay Rd.
715-779-3750

BIG BAY STATE PARK
2402 Hagen Rd.
La Pointe
715-747-6425

FROM BAYFIELD, follow WI-13 W. Turn right onto the US-2 W ramp to Superior.

SS *Meteor*, the World's Last Whaleback Ship

SUPERIOR

Superior's vibe is influenced by the ecosystem of Lake Superior, the largest of the Great Lakes. As one of the Twin Ports, along with Duluth, Minnesota, the city has played a pivotal role in the Great Lakes shipping industry for over a century.

The late 19th and early 20th centuries marked a golden age for Superior. The city's strategic location at the western tip of Lake Superior made it a natural hub for the flourishing iron ore trade. Massive ore carriers, their hulls laden with the precious mineral, arrived in droves, filling the harbor with a constant bustle of activity. Shipyards sprang up to meet the demand for new vessels, and the city's economy thrived.

The construction of the Soo Locks, which bypassed the treacherous rapids of the St. Marys River, further solidified Superior's position as a major shipping center. This engineering marvel opened the Great Lakes to larger vessels, increasing the cargo volume passing through the port.

While the shipping industry has evolved, Superior's maritime heritage remains a cornerstone of its identity. The SS *Meteor*, a restored Great Lakes freighter, serves as a floating museum, offering visitors a firsthand look at the life of a sailor.

Today, Superior continues to be a vital port, handling a diverse range of goods. While the character of the cargo has changed, the spirit of maritime adventure lives on.

Visit!

SUPERIOR ENTRY OBSERVATION AREA AND WISCONSIN POINT LIGHTHOUSE
Wisconsin Point Rd.
715-395-7270

AMNICON FALLS STATE PARK AND HORTON COVERED BRIDGE
4279 Co. Rd. U
South Range
715-398-3000

PATTISON STATE PARK WITH BIG AND LITTLE MANITOU FALLS
6294 WI-35
715-399-3111

BRULE STATE FISH HATCHERY
13847 Hatchery Rd., Brule
715-372-4820

NORTH COUNTRY NATIONAL SCENIC TRAIL—BRULE BOG BOARDWALK
10625 Co. Rd. A
Solon Springs
715-372-5678

TIP

Visit the World of Accordions Museum. This unique institution is the world's largest accordion museum, boasting an impressive collection of over 1,300 accordions from around the globe.

Stay!

SUPERIOR BAY BOUTIQUE MOTEL
306 E Third St.
715-718-2262

ST. CROIX INN
11390 S Fifth St. E Solon Springs
715-378-4444

Living history at Forts Folle Avoine

SIREN

Near Siren, deep in Northwest Wisconsin's Northwoods, Governor Knowles State Forest and Forts Folle Avoine Historical Park offer a captivating escape into nature and history. This dynamic duo provides an unparalleled opportunity to explore the region's natural beauty, immerse oneself in its rich heritage, and embark on unforgettable outdoor adventures.

Governor Knowles State Forest reflects Wisconsin's dedication to preserving its natural heritage. Established in 1970 as the St. Croix River State Forest, it underwent a name change in 1981 to honor former governor Warren P. Knowles, a passionate outdoorsman and conservationist.

to Do!

RICHARD I. BONG VETERANS HISTORICAL CENTER
305 E Second St.
715-392-7151

FAIRLAWN MANSION & MUSEUM
906 E Second St.
715-394-5712

SS METEOR MARITIME MUSEUM
200 Marina Dr. #3285
715-394-5712

OLD FIREHOUSE & POLICE MUSEUM
402 23rd Ave. E #3707
715-394-5712

HARRINGTON ARTS CENTER—WORLD OF ACCORDIONS
1401 Belknap St.
715-395-2787

Eat!

THIRSTY PAGAN BREWING
in the Historic Soo Line Railway Station
1615 Winter St.
715-394-2500

DREAMLAND SUPPER CLUB
4368 Co. Rd. E, South Range
715-398-3706

ANCHOR BAR & GRILL
413 Tower Ave.
715-394-9747

FROM SUPERIOR, head south on Tower Avenue. Take a slight right toward WI-35 S. Merge onto WI-35 S/WI-70 W. Follow into Siren.

TIP

Follow the path of history on the Gandy Dancer Trail. Once a railroad, the track invites cyclists, hikers, and snowmobilers to explore the countryside on the former Soo Line corridor.

Knowles, a staunch advocate for environmental protection, played a pivotal role in developing Wisconsin's state park system. His leadership was instrumental in securing funding for land acquisition and resource management.

Governor Knowles State Forest provides outdoor recreation, while Forts Folle Avoine Historical Park offers historical immersion. This living history museum gives visitors a unique opportunity to experience life as it once was.

The park's name, derived from the French term *folles avoines*, meaning "wild oats," reflects the area's complex history. It was a crossroads where Native American cultures, primarily the Ojibwe, intersected with European fur traders. The park's reconstructed trading posts and Native American dwellings offer a glimpse into this dynamic era.

Visitors to Forts Folle Avoine can step back in time through guided tours, interactive exhibits, and living history demonstrations. Costumed interpreters bring the past to life, sharing stories of the Ojibwe people, French voyageurs, and the challenges of life on the frontier.

Visit!

CREX MEADOWS STATE WILDLIFE AREA
102 E Crex Ave.
Grantsburg
888-936-7463

GOVERNOR KNOWLES STATE FOREST
325 WI-70, Grantsburg
715-463-2898

CCC CAMP RIVERSIDE #626
2Q96+83 (corner of CCC Rd. and Lakes Dr.)
Riverside

Stay!

SMOLAND PRAIRIE HOMESTEAD INN
11658 WI-70, Grantsburg
715-689-2528

THE LODGE AT CROOKED LAKE HOTEL
24271 WI-35
715-349-2500

LILAC VILLAGE BED AND BREAKFAST
7665 Bradley St.
612- 418-6461

Eat!

YELLOW LAKE LODGE
27924 Yellow Lake Rd.
Webster
715-866-4354

JO MAMA'S A&H CORNER CAFÉ
28407 Co. Rd. H, Webster
715-635-2386

CROSSHATCH COFFEE COMPANY
7721 W Main St.
715-349-4090

NORTHVIEW DRIVE-INN
26595 Lakeland Ave.
Webster
715-349-7642

to Do!

BURNETT DAIRY COOPERATIVE CHEESE STORE & BISTRO
11631 WI-70, Grantsburg
715-689-2468

GANDY DANCER STATE TRAIL (SOUTHERN SEGMENT)
7475 WI-77, Danbury
715-349-2157

BRICKFIELD BREWING
130 W Olson Dr.
Grantsburg
715-463-1900

YELLOW RIVER PINBALL
30257 S Glass St., Danbury
612- 419-6852

FORTS FOLLE AVOINE
8500 Co. Hwy. U
Danbury
715-349-8989

HEAD SOUTH ON WI-35 S from Siren. Turn right onto S Road/160th Avenue. Turn left onto 220th Street/ Sunshine Street. Turn right onto Fairgrounds Road. Turn left onto State Road. Turn right onto East Kentucky Street in St. Croix Falls.

ST. CROIX FALLS

The St. Croix River Valley, a pristine expanse straddling the border of Wisconsin and Minnesota, is a haven for nature enthusiasts, history buffs, and adventure seekers alike.

At its heart lies the St. Croix National Scenic Riverway, a protected corridor of unparalleled beauty. Designated a National Scenic Riverway in 1968, the St. Croix River and its tributaries offer a pristine ecosystem. The river's clear waters, flanked by towering sandstone and limestone bluffs, create a breathtaking landscape. Hiking, kayaking, canoeing, and fishing are just a few of the outdoor activities available.

For those seeking a deeper connection with the river, Taylors Falls Scenic Boat Tours offer a unique perspective. These narrated cruises glide through the heart of the Dalles, a stunning stretch of the river characterized by dramatic rock formations and cascading waterfalls. Learn about the area's rich history and geology as you soak in the nature.

Osceola & St. Croix Valley Railway

TIP

Wisconsin's Interstate State Park offers the best views of paddlewheelers navigating the river valley; don't miss the Pothole Trail. The 1,100-mile Ice Age National Scenic Trail starts here.

To complement the river experience, the Osceola & St. Croix Valley Railway invites visitors on a nostalgic journey. This scenic train ride traverses the picturesque St. Croix River Valley, offering magnificent views of the surrounding countryside.

The St. Croix Valley provides a harmonious blend of natural beauty and historical significance. From the rugged wilderness of the National Scenic Riverway to the charming towns along its banks, this region provides a truly unforgettable experience. Whether you're seeking adventure, relaxation, or a glimpse into the past, the St. Croix Valley has something everyone will enjoy.

Eat!

INDIANHEAD SUPPER CLUB
107 Indianhead Shores Dr., Balsam Lake
715-485-3359

DALLES HOUSE RESTAURANT & LOUNGE
720 S Vincent St.
715-483-3246

MILLTOWN DRIVE-IN
125 Main St. W, Milltown
715-825-3389

THE NEW FRONTIER
440 US-8, Turtle Lake
715-986-4797

PURE-N-SIMPLE FARM HOUSE FOODS
867 US-8, Amery
715-268-6800

Visit!

ST. CROIX NATIONAL RIVERWAY VISITOR CENTER
401 N Hamilton St.
715-483-2274

MICHAEL SEVERSEN MEMORIAL OVERLOOK PARK
North Washington St.

POLK COUNTY MUSEUM
120 W Main St.
Balsam Lake
715-485-9269

to Do!

OSCEOLA & ST. CROIX VALLEY RAILWAY
114 Depot Rd., Osceola
651-228-0263

TAYLORS FALLS SCENIC BOAT TOURS
220 South St., Taylors Falls
651-465-6315

FAWN-DOE-ROSA WILDLIFE EDUCATIONAL PARK
2131 US-8
715-483-3772

WILKE GLEN AND CASCADE FALLS
101 N Cascade St., Osceola

ST. CROIX ARTBARN
1040 Oak Ridge Dr., Osceola
715-294-2127

Stay!

ST. CROIX VALLEY INN
305 River St., Osceola
715-494-1677

BIG ROCK CREEK
1674 WI-87
715-501-8172

From St. Croix Falls, follow US-8 E. Take the left exit to US-63N. Continue onto WI-48 E. Stay on WI-48 E. Turn right on Main Street in Rice Lake.

RICE LAKE

In the middle of Red Cedar Lake lies Stout's Island Lodge, a haven where history and modern comfort intertwine. Stout's Island Lodge wasn't built as a resort; it began as a grand family retreat. In 1915, Frank Stout, heir to a lumber fortune, envisioned an exclusive island escape. Transporting cedar logs from Idaho, California redwood, and white pine from nearby dams, he constructed a sprawling 35,000-square-foot compound on his private island. This architectural marvel is decorated with intricate Bavarian

Red Barn Theatre

carvings of pelicans and oak leaves, Gothic arches, and even medieval Norwegian dragon heads, reflecting Stout's extravagant vision.

The renowned Adirondack camps inspired the original main lodge, constructed in 1903. Its interior boasts luxurious touches, including a dining room fireplace adorned with imported Italian stone and a living room fireplace crafted from pink quarry rock from the Hardscrabble Hills. Furthermore, the primary and east islands are joined by a steel bridge, a gift from Andrew Carnegie himself.

Fortunately, Stout's Island Lodge was destined to be found in the passage of time. The meticulously restored lodge and cabins retain their historic charm, while modern amenities are thoughtfully integrated to provide a comfortable escape.

Today, Stout's Island Lodge has eight cabins and two lodge buildings, each possessing its own characteristics. Some cabins boast cozy fireplaces, while others feature private balconies overlooking the glistening lake. Stout's Island Lodge is a chance to reconnect with history, surrounded by the timeless beauty of a bygone era.

Eat!

POKEGAMA LAKESIDE CANTINA
840 Banks Ln., Chetek
715-7641212

LEHMAN'S SUPPER CLUB
2911 S Main St.
715-234-9911

THE BLUEBERRY LINE COFFEE HOUSE
180 N Third St., Barron
715-637-8000

THE COUNTRY SKILLET CAFÉ
1233 Second Ave.
Cumberland
715-822-3462

CHETEK CAFÉ AND MEAT SHOP
505 Second St., Chetek
715-925-2244

LONA'S CORNER CAFÉ
309 Co. Hwy. SS, Haugen
715-234-6110

Stay!

STOUT'S ISLAND LODGE
2799 27th Ave.
Birchwood
715-354-3646

OUTERS RESORT
1748 Pinewood Ave.
Chetek
715-924-3283

SHOREWOOD RESORT
216 Lakeview Dr., Chetek
715-642-0871

Visit!

VETERANS MEMORIAL PARK
600-698 Lakeshore Dr.

LOUIE'S FINER MEATS
2025 Superior Ave.
Cumberland
715-822-4728

to Do!

RED BARN THEATRE
2247 22nd St.
715-234-8301

STARDUST TWIN DRIVE-IN THEATER
995 22nd St., Chetek
715-458-4587

AGONIC BREWING CO.
17C E Messenger St.
715-208-7238

PIONEER VILLAGE MUSEUM
1866 13½ 14th Ave.
Cameron
715-458-2080

TIP

Stout's Island Lodge operates seasonally, welcoming guests from May to the end of October. Reservations are recommended, especially during peak season.

LAKE SUPERIOR
APOSTLE ISLANDS
MICHIGAN
MARQUETTE
WISCONSIN
WASHBURN
ASHLAND
IRONWOOD
CHEQUAMEGON NATIONAL FOREST
HAYWARD
PARK FALLS
LAND O' LAKES
EAGLE RIVER
NICOLET NATIONAL FOREST
KINSFORD
PHILLIPS
RHINELANDER
LADYSMITH
MEDFORD
MERRILL
ANTIGO
MARINETTE
CHIPPEWA FALLS
EAU CLAIRE
OCONTO FALLS
SHAWANO
STURGEON BAY
EGG HARBOR
MARSHFIELD
CLINTONVILLE
MONDOVI
NEILLSVILLE
STEVENS POINT
GREEN BAY
WHITEHALL
WISCONSIN RAPIDS
WAUPACA
BLACK RIVER FALLS
PETENWELL DAM
WAUTOMA
MANITOWOC
TOMAH
CASTLE ROCK LAKE
LAKE WINNEBAGO
LA CROSSE
NEW LISBON
SHEBOYGAN
WESTBY
PORTAGE
BEAVER DAM
RICHLAND CENTER
LAKE MICHIGAN
MENOMONEE FALLS
BOSCOBEL
LAKE MENDOTA
MT. HOREB
MADISON
MILWAUKEE
DODGEVILLE
VERONA
STOUGHTON
NEW GLARUS
LANCASTER
MINERAL POINT
MONROE
JANESVILLE
RACINE
KENOSHA
DUBUQUE
ILLINOIS

MADISON AND HERITAGE TOWNS

A treasure trove of enchanting heritage towns is found in Southern Wisconsin. These towns, each with a unique character and cultural heritage, guarantee a road trip filled with memory-making experiences.

Madison's Capitol, a neoclassical masterpiece, dominates the skyline and is a top tourist attraction where we recommend starting. Take a free guided tour to learn about its beauty and history.

It's easy to see why Mt. Horeb is known as the "Troll Capital of the World" while driving down Main Street. Lifesize wooden hand-carved trolls depicting different scenes adorn both sides of the street. These whimsical carvings are a nod to the town's Scandinavian heritage and its embrace of folklore and fantasy. Stoughton, another small town with a giant Norwegian personality, is well known for its Syttende Mai festival and coffee break tradition.

Mineral Point is a vibrant artistic community that has captivated visitors with its unique blend of history and creativity. The town's historic district, lined with beautifully preserved buildings, is a canvas for local artists. Galleries, studios, and shops showcasing a diverse range of artwork.

In the rolling hills of the Driftless Region, New Glarus, known as "America's Little Switzerland," is a picturesque small town that proudly celebrates its heritage. Visitors can enjoy delicious Swiss cuisine, explore the historic downtown, and experience the unique atmosphere where limburger cheese is still legal tender. Likewise, Monroe, often referred to as the "Swiss Cheese Capital of the USA," is a town that celebrates its rich dairy heritage.

Enjoy a Madison tradition by lounging alongside Lake Mendota in Memorial Union's brightly colored patio chairs.

TO START THE TOUR,

BEGIN IN MADISON on the shores of Lake Mendota at Memorial Union. Drive west to Mt. Horeb and end in Stoughton on this meandering route.

anti-war protests, and environmental activism have all left their mark. This progressive ethos continues to shape the city's identity.

Pop culture has also played a significant role in shaping Madison's image. The city's live music scene is legendary, with venues like the Majestic Theatre hosting diverse artists. Concerts on the Square and live music on the grounds of the state capitol have become nationally recognized events. The Onion, a satirical news publication founded by University of Wisconsin students, has become a global phenomenon.

Madison's blend of history and pop culture has created an intellectually stimulating and culturally vibrant city. With its stunning natural beauty, progressive values, and thriving arts scene, Madison continues to be where people from all walks of life can find their place.

TIP

Madison's Dane County Farmers' Market began in 1972 with just five vendors. It has become the nation's largest producer-only market, inspired by European markets, offering fresh, local produce and goods.

The farmer's market on the square is a favorite of locals and visitors. Courtesy of Tim Manus

Eat!

DOTTY DUMPLING'S DOWRY
317 N Frances St.
608-259-0000

NITTY GRITTY
223 N Frances St.
608-251-2521

MICKIE'S DAIRY BAR
1511 Monroe St.
608-256-9476

MAPLE TREE SUPPER CLUB
6010 US-51, McFarland
608-838-5888

Visit!

MEMORIAL UNION
800 Langdon St.
608-265-3000

CAMP RANDALL STADIUM & MEMORIAL ARCH
1440 Monroe St.
608-262-1866

GEOLOGY MUSEUM
1215 W Dayton St.
608-262-1412

HEAD SOUTH on North Park Street toward West Johnson Street. Turn right onto Regent Street. Turn left onto Monroe Street and slightly left onto Nakoma Road. Turn left onto Midvale Boulevard. Get on US 151/US 18. Take exit 77 for Verona.

to Do!

MADISON ADVENTURE TOURS (DOWNTOWN MADISON E-BIKE TOUR)
600 Williamson St.
608-205-8806

WISCONSIN STATE CAPITOL
2 E Main St.
608-266-0382

HENRY VILAS ZOO
702 S Randall Ave.
608-266-4732

BABCOCK DAIRY STORE
1605 Lindenx Dr.
608-262-3045

Stay!

GRADUATE MADISON
601 Langdon St.
608-257-4391

HOTEL RUBY MARIE
524 E Wilson St.
608-327-7829

MANSION HILL INN
424 N Pinckney St.
608-255-0172

THE LIVINGSTON INN
752 E Gorham St.
608-238-6317

Ride a C. W. Parker Carousel at Epic.

VERONA

The Verona area has a rich history mingled with the broader development of Dane County. Originally inhabited by Native American tribes, the region experienced significant transformation with the arrival of European settlers in the 19th century.

Agriculture became the cornerstone of the local economy, with fertile lands proving ideal for cultivating crops and raising livestock. As the region prospered, small towns like Verona and Paoli emerged as centers of commerce and community. The construction of railroads played a pivotal role in connecting these communities, facilitating trade and transportation and further contributing to the region's growth.

Throughout the 20th century, the area gradually shifted from an agricultural to a more diversified economy. While agriculture remained important, the growth of industries such as manufacturing and technology contributed to the region's development. The proximity to Madison, the state capital, also spurred economic growth and population expansion.

Verona, in particular, has undergone a remarkable transformation in recent decades, evolving from a rural community into a vibrant suburb. This growth is largely attributed to Epic, a global leader in health care software, which has significantly contributed to the area's economic vitality. Even Paoli, while retaining its rural charm, has reaped the benefits of the region's overall prosperity.

Verona has a high quality of life, combining the tranquility of small-town living with the conveniences of urban amenities. With its strong sense of community, excellent schools, and abundant recreational opportunities, the area continues to attract residents and visitors alike.

TIP

Epic's Verona campus houses a historic 1927 C. W. Parker carousel, once part of Madison's Ella's Deli; rescued and restored by Epic in 2018, it continues to enchant visitors.

Eat!

THE RILEY TAVERN
8205 Klevenville-Riley Rd.
608-845-9150

AVANTIS ITALIAN RESTAURANT & PUB
119 Main St.
608-848-3315

GUS'S DINER
110 Keenan Ct.
608-497-0230

QUIVEY'S GROVE
6261 Nesbitt Rd., Fitchburg
608-273-4900

to Do!

THE SOW'S EAR
125 S Main St.
608-848-2755

LAKE LOUIE BREWING
1079 American Way
608-845-1327

BAVARIA SAUSAGE
6317 Nesbitt Rd., Fitchburg
608-271-1295

HOP GARDEN BREWERY
6889 Canal St., Belleville
608-636-6229

Stay!

INN AT SEVEN ACRE
6858 Paoli Rd., Belleville
608-416-4023

CAMEO ROSE VICTORIAN COUNTRY INN
1090 Severson Rd.
Belleville
608-424-6340

Visit!

PRAIRIE MORAINE COUNTY PARK
6679 Wesner Ln., Epic

1979 MILKY WAY
608-271-9000

THE FARLEY CENTER
2299 Spring Rose Rd.
608-845-8724

LANDMARK CREAMERY PROVISIONS
6895 Paoli Rd., Belleville
608-848-1162

PAOLI SCHOOLHOUSE AMERICAN BISTRO
6857 Paoli Rd., Belleville
608-848-6261

Epic offers whimsical tours of its campus.

TAKE US-151S/US-18 W. Take exit 75 toward County Highway G, turn left on County Highway G. Turn right onto WI-92 Trunk E to Mount Horeb.

MOUNT HOREB

Surrounded by the rolling hills of farmland in the Driftless Region, the small town of Mount Horeb is known for its rich Norwegian heritage. Mount Horeb has evolved from a quiet farming community to a destination known as the "Troll Capital of the World."

The town's history traces back to the Ho-Chunk Native American people who originally inhabited the land. European settlers arrived in the mid-19th century, drawn by the region's natural beauty and fertile soil. The town's name, inspired by the biblical Mount Horeb, was adopted in 1861, reflecting the community's strong religious ties.

Mount Horeb's metamorphosis into a troll-themed wonderland began in the 1970s. A local shop's decision to display imported troll figurines sparked a magical transformation. These whimsical creatures captured the hearts of the community, inspiring local artisans to create their own unique troll sculptures. Mount Horeb wholeheartedly embraced the troll theme.

The town's commitment to its trollish identity has grown exponentially. The Trollway, a delightful trail showcasing a diverse collection of troll sculptures, has become a must-see attraction for visitors from around the world. Local businesses have incorporated the troll theme into their products and services, creating a truly immersive experience.

Today, Mount Horeb is a thriving community that celebrates its troll heritage while preserving its history. The town's ability to blend tradition with whimsy has made it a beloved destination for families, art enthusiasts, and those seeking an enjoyable and unforgettable experience.

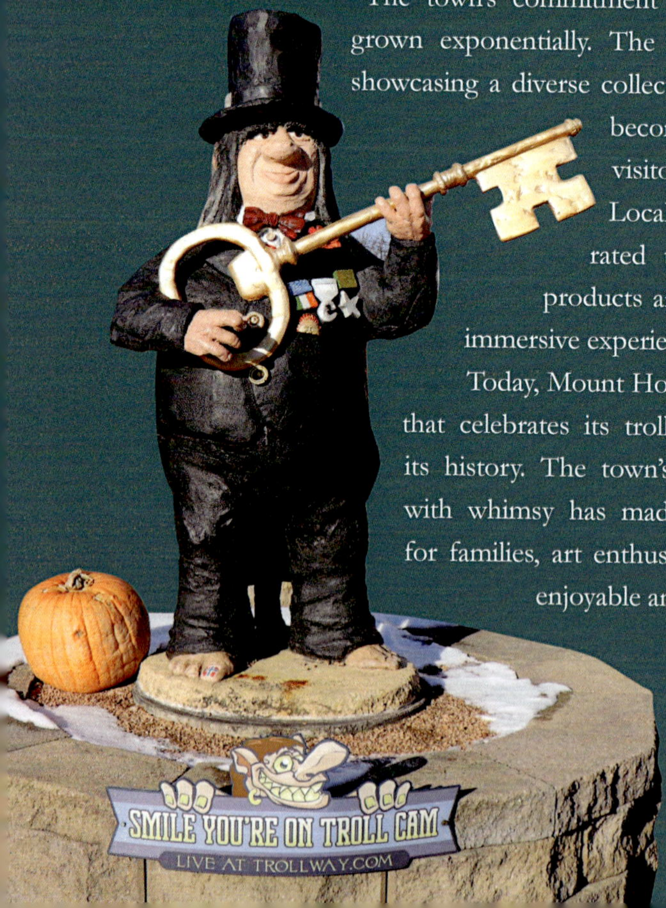

Just one of the trolls along the Tollway in Mount Horeb

Experience Norwegian heritage and culture in Mount Horeb.

TIP

District #1 Old Schoolhouse, built in 1889, is Mount Horeb's oldest standing schoolhouse. Restored and relocated, it's a local landmark hosting events and educational programs.

Eat!

HOFF BISTRO 101
101 E Main St.
608-437-9463

GRUMPY TRAIL BREWPUB
105 S Second St.
608-437-2739

FINK'S RESTAURANT
204 W Main St.
608-437-8922

Stay!

CLARENCE GONSTEAD GUEST COTTAGE
602 S Second St.
608-437-4374

SUNNIVA INN
120 N Grove St.
608-437-4427

BRIGHAM FARMHOUSE
2990 Cave of The Mounds Rd.
Blue Mounds
608-234-8047

Visit!

DONALD COUNTY PARK
1945 State Hwy. 92

STEWART LAKE COUNTY PARK
3106 Co. Hwy. JG
608-224-3730

BLUE MOUNDS STATE PARK
4350 Mounds Park Rd.
Blue Mounds
608-437-5711

MILITARY RIDGE STATE TRAIL
116 S Second St.

to Do!

OPEN HOUSE IMPORTS
308 E Main St.
608-437-5468

CENTER GROUND STUDIOS
302 E Lincoln St.
920-299-2368

CAVE OF THE MOUNDS
2975 Cave of the Mounds Rd., Blue Mounds
608-437-3038

WALLY KELLER TOOL MUSEUM
100 W Main St.
608-437-8655

TYROL BASIN
3487 Bohn Rd.
608-437-4135

FROM MOUNT HOREB, take Highway ID/ County Road ID to Barneveld. **FROM BARNEVELD,** take US-151 S/18 W. Turn right onto County Highway Y/ YZ to Dodgeville.

DODGEVILLE

Dodgeville exists because of the rugged beauty and mineral wealth of the Driftless Area. Named after Henry Dodge, a prominent figure in Wisconsin's early history, the town emerged as a bustling mining center in the early 19th century.

Dodge, a military officer and later the first governor of the Wisconsin Territory, played a pivotal role in the region's development. His influence is evident in the town's name and the nearby Governor Dodge State Park.

Dodgeville experienced rapid growth during the lead mining boom. The town's strategic location and access to mineral resources made it a thriving center for trade and commerce. While mining eventually declined, Dodgeville managed to preserve its historical charm. Today, visitors can explore the town's heritage through its well-preserved architecture and local museums.

Governor Dodge State Park, located just outside Dodgeville, offers a stunning contrast to the town's historic roots. The park showcases the natural beauty of the Driftless Area.

The park was established in 1948 and has since grown to encompass over 5,000 acres of rolling hills, deep valleys, and sparkling lakes. Hiking, camping, fishing, and other outdoor activities are popular pastimes within the park. Visitors can explore the park and its remnants of the area's mining past.

Together, Dodgeville and Governor Dodge State Park provide a unique blend of history and nature, making this region a captivating destination for travelers seeking a taste of Wisconsin's past and present.

Don Q Inn

Try an old-fashioned peanut bar at Quality Bakery on Main Street.

TIP

Dodgeville celebrates the humble grilled cheese with its annual Wisconsin Grilled Cheese Championship. Enjoy live music, family fun, and a variety of cheesy creations.

Eat!

BOB'S BITCHIN' BBQ
167 N Iowa St.
608-930-2227

QUALITY BAKERY
154 N Iowa St.
608-935-3812

HI POINT STEAKHOUSE
6900 Co. Rd. HHH
Ridgeway
608-924-2819

RED ROOM BAR & RESTAURANT
108 E Merrimac St.
608-935-7108

Stay!

HOUSE ON THE ROCK RESORT
400 Springs Dr.
Spring Green
608-935-3639

DON Q INN
3658 State Hwy. 23 N
608-367-5161

BLACKHAWK LAKE RECREATION AREA
2025 Co. Hwy. BH
Highland
608-623-2707

to Do!

HOUSE ON THE ROCK
5754 State Hwy. 23
Spring Green
608-935-3639

FOLKLORE VILLAGE
3210 Co. Rd. BB
608-924-4000

ADAMAH ART STUDIOS
4681 Co. Rd. ZZ
608-574-9693

TALIESIN
5481 Co. Rd. C
Spring Green
608-588-7900

DODGE POINT COUNTRY CLUB
1771 Co. Rd. YD
Mineral Point
608-987-2500

WYOMING VALLEY SCHOOL CULTURAL ARTS CENTER
6306 Hwy. 23
Spring Green
608-588-2544

Visit!

WHITE OAK SAVANNA FARM & SANCTUARY
4352 State Hwy. 23
608-636-5776

GOVERNOR DODGE STATE PARK
4175 State Hwy. 23
608-935-2315

FROM DODGEVILLE, head south on WI-23. Take the WI-23 S/US-151 S ramp to Mineral Point/Dubuque. Take exit 40 for WI-23 S toward WI-39/US 151 Business/Mineral Point.

MINERAL POINT

Mineral Point, an artistic town in Wisconsin's Driftless Area, was created with the allure of mineral wealth. Cornish immigrants arrived in the early 19th century, drawn by the promise of lead and zinc ore. These hardy miners brought their distinctive culture and unique building style, which are still evident in the town's character.

The mining boom propelled Mineral Point into a thriving commercial center. Its abundant mineral resources fostered economic growth. The town's streets were filled with bustling activity as miners, merchants, and settlers converged.

However, the mining industry's decline in the late 19th century forced Mineral Point to adapt. Today, visitors can experience its historical charm and wander through its well-preserved streets, admiring the Cornish stone cottages that dot the landscape.

One of Mineral Point's most iconic areas is Shake Rag. This historic neighborhood, rumored to be named for the practice of women shaking rags to signal mealtime to their husbands working in the nearby mines, is a treasure trove of history. The Cornish miners built their stone cottages in this area, creating a unique architectural landscape that has been carefully preserved.

TIP

Located on Highway 39, Nick Engelbert's Grandview is a whimsical outdoor art museum featuring concrete sculptures and mosaics. This unique property showcases the imagination of a self-taught artist.

Downtown Mineral Point

Sirius Sunlight Glass Studio, downtown Mineral Point

Mineral Point has preserved its heritage and embraced it, transforming into an energetic tourist destination. The town's history and artistic flair have attracted a community of artists and craftsmen. Visitors can explore charming shops, indulge in local cuisine, and immerse themselves in the town's distinctive atmosphere.

Eat!

POINTER CAFÉ
809 Ridge St.
608-987-3733

RED ROOSTER CAFÉ
158 High St.
608-987-9936

MIDWAY BAR AND GRILL
140 High St.
608-987-4309

Visit!

PENDARVIS
114 Shakerag St.
608-987-2122

MINERAL POINT RAILROAD MUSEUM
11 Commerce St.
608-987-2695

WISCONSIN ODD FELLOW REBEKAH MUSEUM
112 Front St.

Stay!

COMMERCE STREET BREWERY HOTEL
23 Commerce St.
608-987-3298

MINERAL POINT HOTEL & SUITES
121 Commerce St.
608-987-3889

COTTAGE ON CHESTNUT
99 N Chestnut St.
608-553-1979

WALKER HOUSE
1 Water St.
608-553-0728

to Do!

THE BOOK KITCHEN—COOKING & COMMUNITY
151 High St.

HOOK'S CHEESE CO.
320 Commerce St.
608-987-3259

SHAKE RAG ALLEY CENTER FOR THE ARTS
18 Shakerag St.
608-987-3292

MINERAL POINT OPERA HOUSE
139 High St.
608-987-3501

SIRIUS SUNLIGHT GLASS STUDIO
218 High St.
608-987-2716

FROM MINERAL POINT, take WI-39 E/WI-39 Trunk E. Turn left onto WI-39 E/WI-78 N to New Glarus.

NEW GLARUS

New Glarus stands as an example of the enduring spirit of Swiss heritage. Founded in 1845 by a group of Swiss immigrants seeking religious and economic freedom, the town has meticulously preserved its European roots.

These pioneers brought a rich tapestry of culture, traditions, and agricultural expertise. They transformed the rugged wilderness into a thriving community, introducing Swiss crops and livestock to the region. The distinctive Swiss chalet-style architecture adorning the landscape is a tangible reminder of their European origins.

A cornerstone of New Glarus's identity is the annual Wilhelm Tell Festival, a colorful celebration of Swiss heritage. This event, which draws visitors from far and wide, provides an exceptional opportunity to experience traditional Swiss music, dance, and cuisine. The festival is a powerful reminder of the deep-rooted connection between the village and its Swiss ancestry and a highlight for those seeking an authentic cultural experience.

Beyond the annual festivities, the Swiss influence permeates daily life in New Glarus. From the local bakeries offering authentic Swiss pastries to the cheesemakers producing artisanal cheeses, the town presents a genuine taste of Switzerland. The community's unwavering commitment to preserving its heritage is evident in the meticulous care taken to maintain traditions and customs. This dedication ensures that future generations will appreciate the legacy of the Swiss pioneers, and it makes New Glarus a captivating Swiss cultural destination.

Eat!

TOFFLERS PUB & GRILL
200 Fifth Ave.
608-527-2490

GLARNER STUBE
518 First St.
608-527-2216

KING BUBBA'S DINER & SPIRITS
244 N Main St.
Monticello
608-938-1385

Stay!

CHALET LANDHAUS INN
801 WI-69
608-527-5234

THE BLANC CHALET
1200 WI-69
608-527-2138

ALBANY HOUSE
Psalms Way, Albany
608-862-3636

ROSE HILL COUNTRY INN
8520 Zentner Rd.
608-527-5320

TIP

New Glarus Brewery offers exclusive three-hour Hard Hat Tours. Your brewery ambassador will guide you on a behind-the-scenes tour of both breweries, followed by a private beer and cheese pairing.

Visit!

CHALET OF THE GOLDEN FLEECE MUSEUM
618 Second St.
608-527-2614

NEW GLARUS WOODS STATE PARK
W5446 Co. Hwy. NN
608-527-2335

NEW GLARUS BAKERY
534 First St.
608-527-2916

SWISS HISTORICAL VILLAGE MUSEUM
612 Seventh Ave.
608-527-2317

SUGAR RIVER STATE TRAIL
W5508 Co. Hwy. NN

to Do!

NEW GLARUS BREWING COMPANY
2400 WI-69
608-527-5850

S & B TUBING
100 E Main St., Albany
608-862-3933

SILVER LEWIS CHEESE FACTORY
W3075 Co. Hwy. EE
Monticello
608-938-4813

FROM NEW GLARUS,
take US-69 S to Monroe.

MONROE

The town's remarkable transformation from a mining settlement to a dairy and cheese powerhouse showcases the perseverance and dedication of the Swiss immigrants who arrived in the mid-19th century.

These skilled dairy farmers brought with them centuries-old cheesemaking traditions. They established farmstead cheese factories, where milk from their herds was transformed into various kinds of cheese, including Swiss, brick, and Limburger. As demand grew, cooperative cheese factories emerged, given Monroe's position as a cheesemaking center.

By the early 20th century, Monroe produced millions of pounds of cheese annually. The town's reputation as the "Cheese Capital of the USA" was firmly established. While the number of cheese factories has declined, Monroe's legacy as a cheesemaking hub endures.

Today, the National Historic Cheesemaking Center Museum gives visitors a fascinating experience, providing a glimpse into the region's cheesemaking history. It houses restored cheesemaking equipment and showcases the evolution of the industry.

The Cheese Days festival, a cornerstone of Monroe's cheese heritage, celebrates the region's rich cultural history. It attracts thousands of visitors and showcases the best of the region's cheese, music, food, and entertainment.

Monroe has capitalized on its fame by developing a robust cheese tourism industry. Visitors can enjoy cheese tours, cheesemaking demonstrations, and ample opportunities to sample local cheeses.

TIP

Baumgartner's Cheese Store & Tavern is the iconic spot to experience a traditional Limburger cheese sandwich. Even with its pungent odor, it's a unique and, some say, tasty Wisconsin experience.

Eat!

BAUMGARTNER'S CHEESE STORE & TAVERN
1023 16th Ave.
608-325-6157

BENNETT'S JUNCTION HOUSE
N3693 Co. Hwy. J
608-325-2808

RATSKELLER RESTAURANT
1217 17th Ave.
608-325-3461

Visit!

CHALET CHEESE COOPERATIVE
N4858 Co. Hwy. N
608-325-4343

ALP & DELL CHEESE STORE
657 Second St.
608-328-3355

DECATUR DAIRY
W1668 Co. Hwy. F
Brodhead
608-897-8661

NATIONAL HISTORIC CHEESEMAKING CENTER MUSEUM
2108 Sixth Ave.
608-325-4636

Stay!

GASTHAUS MOTEL
685 30th St.
608-328-8395

REIDERHOUSE
2023 13th St.

THE DAIRY AT WEGMUELLER FARM
W4358 Montgomery Rd.
608-293-2340

SUGAR RIVER LOFT
929 W Exchange St.
Brodhead
608-214-6851

to Do!

KELCH AVIATION MUSEUM
N2463 Airport Rd., Brodhead
608-897-1175

THE TOY BARN MUSEUM
W9141 WI-81, Argyle
608-897-5651

GOETZ SKY-VU DRIVE IN
N1936 WI-69
608-325-4545

TURNER HALL OF MONROE
(Sunday Dances)
1217 17th Ave.

TAKE WI-59 E. Turn left onto WI-59 E/County Highway E. Turn left onto WI-104 N/WI-59 E. Right on WI-59. Left on North County Road M. Left on Tolles Road. Continue onto WI-138 N Trunk N to Stoughton.

STOUGHTON

Stoughton is renowned for its deep-rooted Norwegian heritage. The city's story is inextricably linked to the waves of Norwegian immigrants who arrived in the late 19th century, seeking economic opportunities in farming and manufacturing.

Norwegian culture permeated every aspect of life in early Stoughton. The language was widely spoken, and Norwegian customs and traditions became the fabric of the community. Scandinavian influences shaped the town's character from traditional architecture to folk art and music.

A cornerstone of Stoughton's Norwegian identity is the annual Syttende Mai festival, a colorful celebration of Norway's Constitution Day. This citywide event is a demonstration of the enduring pride in Norwegian heritage. Witness all things Norwegian, from dance to food to music to history.

While fewer people speak Norwegian in Stoughton these days, the legacy lives on. The Livsreise Norwegian Heritage Center is committed to preserving and sharing the stories of Norwegian immigrants. Through exhibits, genealogy resources, and cultural programs, the center helps to keep the spirit of Norway alive.

Downtown Stoughton

Rosemaling exhibit at the annual Syttende Mai Festival

Today, Stoughton is a harmonious blend of old and new, where Norwegian heritage coexists with modern life. The city's Scandinavian roots continue to be a source of pride and inspiration.

TIP

The Wisconsin State Rosemaling Association was founded in Stoughton in 1967. Today, it offers classes throughout the year and hosts an exhibition and sale during Syttende Mai.

Eat!

FOSDAL HOME BAKERY
243 E Main St.
608-873-3073

KOFFEE KUP
355 E Main St.
608-873-6717

VIKING BREW PUB
211 E Main St.
608-719-5041

SUNRISE FAMILY RESTAURANT
1052 W Main St.
608-877-1930

Stay!

ALTEMUS CORNERS HOUSE
1345 Tower Dr.
608-695-0693

NAESET-ROE BED & BREAKFAST
126 E Washington St.
608-877-4150

Visit!

STOUGHTON HISTORICAL SOCIETY MUSEUM
324 S Page St.
608-873-4797

LIVSREISE NORWEGIAN HERITAGE CENTER
277 W Main St.
608-873-7567

LAKE KEGONSA STATE PARK
2405 Door Creek Rd.

to Do!

EUGSTER'S FARM MARKET
3865 WI-138
608-873-3822

NORDIC NOOK
176 W Main St.
608-877-0848

YAHARA CHOCOLATE
261 W Main St.
608-205-9500

STOUGHTON OPERA HOUSE
381 E Main St.
608-877-4400

STOUGHTON VILLAGE PLAYERS THEATER
255 E Main St.
608-492-0720

CHEESERS
183 E Main St.
608-873-1777

LAKE SUPERIOR
APOSTLE ISLANDS
MICHIGAN
MARQUETTE
WASHBURN
ASHLAND
IRONWOOD
CHEQUAMEGON NATIONAL FOREST
HAYWARD
PARK FALLS
LAND O' LAKES
EAGLE RIVER
NICOLET NATIONAL FOREST
KINSFORD
PHILLIPS
RHINELANDER
LADYSMITH
MEDFORD
MERRILL
ANTIGO
WISCONSIN
MARINETTE
OCONTO FALLS
SHAWANO
STURGEON BAY
EGG HARBOR
GREEN BAY
MARSHFIELD
CLINTONVILLE
ONDOVI
NEILLSVILLE
STEVENS POINT
WHITEHALL
WISCONSIN RAPIDS
WAUPACA
APPLETON
BLACK RIVER FALLS
PETENWELL DAM
NEENAH
MANITOWOC
RIVER
WAUTOMA
OSHKOSH
TOMAH
CASTLE ROCK LAKE
LAKE WINNEBAGO
LA CROSSE
NEW LISBON
FOND DU LAC
SHEBOYGAN
PLYMOUTH
WESTBY
PORTAGE
BEAVER DAM
WEST BEND
RICHLAND CENTER
HARTFORD
MENOMONEE FALLS
LAKE MICHI
BOSCOBEL
LAKE MENDOTA
GLENDALE
MADISON
MILWAUKEE
DODGEVILLE
STOUGHTON
LANCASTER
JANESVILLE
RACINE
MONROE
KENOSHA
DUBUQUE
ILLINOIS

LAKE WINNEBAGO REGION:

INNOVATIONS AND A CHEESE LOVER'S PARADISE

Get out of the city on a road trip around Lake Winnebago, the largest lake entirely in Wisconsin. An excellent place to begin your road trip would be in Hubertus at the impressive Holy Hill Basilica. This sacred site has been a place of pilgrimage and reflection for centuries. The hill is a natural marvel, offering breathtaking panoramic views of the surrounding countryside. Visitors can hike or drive to the summit, where the towering basilica and a peaceful atmosphere will greet them. The serene setting and the site's spiritual significance create a truly memorable experience.

However, don't miss the Wisconsin Automotive Museum in Hartford, a haven for car enthusiasts and home to a vast collection of vintage automobiles, including a notable collection from Hartford's Kissel Motor Car Company (1906–1931). Amelia Earhart enjoyed road trips in her Kissel Gold Bug Speedster across the United States and Canada.

Embrace your inner child by going to Fond du Lac's Lakeside Park, a beautiful park with amusement rides. Afterward, devour frozen custard at Gilles. The Gilles Fond du Lac location was established in 1949, and just like in its heyday, you have to turn your headlights on for service.

While Appleton is renowned for its role in developing hydroelectric power and for Harry Houdini, Plymouth, on the eastern side of Lake Winnebago, is a cheese lover's paradise. Visit the huge *Antoinette Dairy Cow* statue, a popular roadside attraction, and the "Cheese Capital of the World" arch.

TO START THE TOUR, HOLY HILL IN HUBERTUS and drive clockwise around Lake Winnebago ending in Glendale.

Scoop DeVille Ice Cream Shop

HARTFORD

A significant chapter in Hartford's history involves the Kissel Motor Car Company, which operated from 1903 to 1931. The company was a cornerstone of Hartford's industrial history. Founded by Louis Kissel and his sons in 1906, the company quickly gained a reputation for producing high-quality automobiles. Kissel cars were popular among discerning buyers who knew them for their innovative designs and robust engines.

While the Kissel Motor Car Company made a range of vehicles, four models stand out. The Kissel Kar, the company's flagship model, was known for its luxurious interior and powerful engine. However, the Kissel Speedster, a sportier variant of the Kissel Kar, appealed to those seeking performance and style.

TIP

The city's automotive heritage is celebrated at the Wisconsin Automotive Museum, showcasing a remarkable collection of Kissel vehicles and other classic cars.

Perhaps Kissel's most popular model was the Gold Bug. Amelia Earhart, the pioneering aviator, owned a Kissel Gold Bug Speedster, a reflection of her adventurous spirit. This iconic car, known for its speed and style, accompanied her on cross-country road trips. Earhart's ownership of the Kissel added to the car's legendary status, making it a coveted collectible among automobile enthusiasts. In addition to passenger cars, Kissel produced a line of trucks that were well-regarded for their durability and power.

The company's success contributed significantly to Hartford's growth and prosperity. However, the challenges of the Great Depression forced the Kissel Motor Car Company to cease operations in 1931. While the company's production ended, its legacy lives on through the passion of car enthusiasts and the preservation of its vehicles.

Eat!

SCOOP DEVILLE ICE CREAM SHOP
65 N Main St.
262-673-1957

PENNY'S ERIN RESTAURANT & MOTEL
911 WI-83
262-966-1050

THE FOX & HOUNDS RESTAURANT
1298 Friess Lake Rd.
Hubertus
262-628-1111

LITTLE RED INN
4900 WI-175
262-644-8181

ALPINE RETREAT
1380 Friess Lake Rd.
Hubertus
262-628-3995

PERC PLACE
43 N Main St.
262-670-6950

to Do!

HOLY HILL—BASILICA AND NATIONAL SHRINE OF MARY HELP OF CHRISTIANS
1525 Carmel Rd.
Hubertus
262-628-1838

HOLY HILL TRAILHEAD—ICE AGE NATIONAL SCENIC TRAIL SEGMENT
5856-5898 Donegal Rd.
Hubertus

WISCONSIN AUTOMOTIVE MUSEUM
147 N Rural St.
262-673-7999

KETTLE MORAINE PLAYHOUSE
204 Kettle Moraine Dr. S
Slinger
262-223-6061

RICHFIELD HISTORICAL PARK
1896 WI-164, Richfield

EDWARD H. WOLF SCHLEISINGERVILLE TO SLINGER HISTORICAL MUSEUM
414 Kettle Moraine Dr. S
Slinger
262-297-1580

ICE AGE NATIONAL SCENIC TRAIL—MONCHES SEGMENT
Intersection of County Line Rd. and Kettle Moraine Scenic Dr.

FROM HARTFORD, turn left onto West State Street. Turn right onto County Road P. At the traffic circle, take the second exit and stay on County Road P. Turn left onto WI-175 N/W-67 into Fond Du Lac.

Stay!

BED AND BREAKFAST GARDEN HOUSE
3145 Western Ave., Jackson
262-677-9799

Visit!

POWDER HILL OBSERVATION TOWER
600 Powder Hill Rd.

FOND DU LAC

Fond du Lac played a pivotal role in the early days of Wisconsin statehood. In 1836, when the Wisconsin Territory was established, there was a heated debate over the location of the capital. Fond du Lac was nearly chosen, losing by a single vote to Madison.

While Fond du Lac narrowly missed becoming the state capital, the city later became the birthplace of a revolutionary inventor, King Camp Gillette. The Safety Razor Company, founded in 1901, became a household name, transforming the shaving industry and securing Gillette's place in history. Inspired by the disposable nature of bottle caps, Gillette envisioned a razor blade that could be easily replaced. After years of experimentation and overcoming numerous setbacks, he finally patented his design in 1904.

While Gillette's innovation revolutionized personal care, the architectural landscape also evolved. Built in 1923, the Hotel Retlaw was designed in neoclassical style by Milwaukee hotelier Walter Schroeder. The hotel's name is a backward spelling of its owner's first name.

While the luxury hotel took shape, a different kind of enterprise emerged in rural Wisconsin. Swiss immigrant John O. Widmer founded Widmer's Cheese Cellars in Theresa in 1922. Renowned for its high-quality brick cheese, the company has maintained its tradition for generations. The Widmer family uses John's original bricks to press the cheese and honors his legacy by producing cheese according to the original recipe.

Lakeside Park

Rock around the clock at Gilles.

TIP

After visiting Widmer's, stop by Confections for any Occasion for a wide variety of handmade chocolates and many of those hard-to-find nostalgic candies from your childhood.

Eat!

GILLES FROZEN CUSTARD
819 S Main St.
920-922-4900

THE DINER
175 S Main St.
920-921-9660

CELLAR DISTRICT
40 E Division St.
920-238-9721

BRICK HOUSE
161 S Main St.
920-933-5230

SALTY'S SEAFOOD & SPIRITS
503 N Park Ave.
920-922-9940

KELLEY COUNTRY CREAMERY
W5215 Co. Rd. B
920-923-1715

RED CABIN AT GREEN ACRES
W2701 Fourth St. Rd.
Co. Rd. T
920-906-9110

to Do!

LAKESIDE PARK RIDES
555 N Park Ave.
920-322-3460

FOND DU LAC COUNTY HISTORICAL SOCIETY—BLAKELY MUSEUM
336 Old Pioneer Rd.
920-922-1166

GALLOWAY HOUSE & VILLAGE TOURS
336 Old Pioneer Rd.
920-922-1166

WIDMER'S CHEESE CELLARS
214 W Henni St., Theresa
888-878-1107

CONFECTIONS FOR ANY OCCASION
101 N Milwaukee St.
Theresa
920-488-9269

Stay!

HOTEL RETLAW
1 N Main St.
920-204-0400

Visit!

SOLOMON JUNEAU HOUSE
201 S Milwaukee St., Theresa

FOND DU LAC LIGHTHOUSE
Lighthouse Dr.

FROM MAIN STREET, turn left on Western Avenue. Turn right onto South Brooke Street. Turn left onto West Scott Street. Turn right onto US-45 N. Turn left onto Algoma Boulevard. Turn right onto I-41 ALT/Jackson Street in Oshkosh.

Military Veterans Museum

TIP

Step back in time at Ardy & Ed's Drive-In. Enjoy classic American food served by roller-skating carhops while grooving to '50s tunes. It's a must-visit for a nostalgic experience.

OSHKOSH

Oshkosh is known by aviation enthusiasts worldwide due to the Experimental Aircraft Association (EAA) AirVenture. Founded in 1953, the EAA began as a gathering for home aircraft builders. The event outgrew its early locations, eventually finding a permanent home in Oshkosh in 1970. Since then, EAA AirVenture has grown exponentially, attracting hundreds of thousands of visitors annually. Oshkosh has become the epicenter of the aviation world, hosting everything from experimental aircraft to historical warbirds.

From the heights of aviation to the ground beneath our feet, Oshkosh has diverse experiences. The Military Veterans Museum & Education Center features an impressive collection of military vehicles, including a replica of the Brutus gun truck and an LCVP (Higgins) boat.

While the museum gives a poignant look at the past, the Grand Oshkosh provides a glimpse into the city's architectural heritage. The Grand Oshkosh is a Victorian-era theater from 1883 that boasts stunning details. The interior contains original features, including ornate plasterwork, a magnificent chandelier, a hand-painted drop curtain, and a beautifully restored stage.

Eat!

LEON'S FROZEN CUSTARD
121 W Murdock Ave.
920-231-7755

ARDY & ED'S DRIVE IN
2413 S Main St.
920-231-5455

THE ROXY SUPPER CLUB
571 N Main St.
920-231-1980

WENDT'S ON THE LAKE
N9699 Lakeshore Dr.
Van Dyne
920-688-5231

WHITE HOUSE INN
5776 Main St.
Butte des Morts
920-582-7211

THE WELL DRIVE-IN
705 E Main St.
Winneconne
920-582-7292

to Do!

EAA AVIATION MUSEUM
3000 Poberenzy Rd.
920-426-4800

WINNEBAGO COUNTY HISTORICAL & ARCHAEOLOGICAL SOCIETY
234 Church Ave.
920-267-8007

OSHKOSH PUBLIC MUSEUM
1331 Algoma Blvd.
920-236-5799

PAINE ART CENTER & GARDENS
1410 Algoma Blvd.
920-235-6903

MILITARY VETERANS MUSEUM
4300 Poberezny Rd.
920-426-8615

THE GRAND OSHKOSH
100 High Ave.
920-424-2350

HUGHES' HOME MAID CHOCOLATES SHOP
1823 Doty St.
920-231-7232

Stay!

BRAYWOOD INN
143 Church Ave.
920-309-6350

Visit!

TRIBAL HERITAGE CROSSING TRAIL
Highway 41
Lake Butte des Morts

The popular Osh Vegas sign in Oshkosh

As the Grand Oshkosh displays a feast for the eyes, another local gem delights the taste buds. Hughes' Home Maid Chocolates has been an Oshkosh sweet spot since the 1920s. The Hughes family began crafting their renowned confections in that decade, turning their passion into an official business in 1942. This charming chocolate shop is discreetly located in a bungalow basement. Enter through the side door to discover a world of chocolate delights.

HEAD NORTH ON US-41 ALT/JACKSON STREET. Turn right onto West New York Avenue. Turn left onto North Main Street. Turn right onto Harrison Street. Turn left onto West Doty Avenue, arriving in Neenah.

Timeless charm in downtown Neenah

NEENAH

Although the Fox River powered Neenah's industrial growth, the city's architectural heritage is equally impressive. The Neenah Clock Tower, formerly the Old City Hall, is a prominent landmark in the city's heart. Built in 1881 in the Second Empire architectural style, the structure served as the city's government center for many years.

While Neenah boasts its impressive clock tower, the neighboring town of Menasha has a different historical perspective. The Tayco Street Bridge Tower Museum in Menasha provides an opportunity to step back in time. The museum showcases Menasha's early transportation history, including its water and land systems.

As the museum delves into the past, another local business focuses on the present. Union Star Cheese Factory has been a Metzig family business since its founding in 1911. Now in its fourth generation of ownership, Union Star continues to produce high-quality cheese. Visitors can watch cheesemaking firsthand, as the store is part of the cheese factory.

Eat!

CANNOVA'S PIZZERIA
113 W Wisconsin Ave.
920-886-0325

THE OLD GROG
546 Broad St., Menasha
920-215-6525

GREENE'S POUR HOUSE
134 W Wisconsin Ave.
920-486-1049

CRANKY PAT'S PIZZA
905 S Commercial St.
920-725-2662

EMPRIZE BREW MILL
200 Main St., Menasha
920-486-1539

to Do!

WEIS EARTH SCIENCE MUSEUM
1478 Midway Rd., Menasha
920-832-2925

BERGSTROM-MAHLER MUSEUM OF GLASS
165 N Park Ave.
920-751-4658

TAYCO STREET BRIDGE TOWER MUSEUM
98 Center St., Menasha

UNION STAR CHEESE FACTORY
7742 Co. Rd. II, Fremont
920-836-2804

TIP

Discover stunning glass art at the free Bergstrom-Mahler Museum of Glass. It's a glass lover's paradise, with everything from antique paperweights to modern masterpieces.

Visit!

OLD CITY HALL/NEENAH CLOCK TOWER
206 S Commercial St.

KIMBERLY POINT PARK
290 Lakeshore Ave.
920-886-6060

ISLE OF VALOR
640 Keyes St., Menasha

SMITH PARK
301 Park St., Menasha
920-967-3640

Stay!

THE HOTEL FREMONT
218 Wolf River Dr., Fremont
920-446-2402

WILLOW BEND BED & BREAKFAST
E5490 N Shore Rd., Weyauwega
715-498-9591

Weyauwega Star Dairy is another family-owned option. Established in 1975 by Jim Knaus, the dairy has produced high-quality, handcrafted Italian cheeses for generations. Known for its Parmesan, Asiago, and Romano, Star Dairy has become another favorite cheesemaker renowned for its commitment to traditional methods and exceptional taste. Knaus's passion for cheese extended beyond quality. In 1995, he set a Guinness World Record by creating a 1.5-mile-long string cheese that locals carried through town.

HEAD NORTHWEST on West Doty Avenue toward South Church Street. Turn left onto Main Street. Turn right onto North Lake Street. Turn right to stay on North Lake Street. Turn left onto Stroebe Road. Turn right onto Northern Road. Turn right onto West Prospect Avenue. Turn left onto South State Street in Appleton.

APPLETON

Appleton holds a significant place in the history of hydroelectric power in the United States. In 1882, the Vulcan Street Plant, the world's first commercial hydroelectric power station, began operating.

While the Vulcan Street Plant revolutionized power generation, the Hearthstone Historic House Museum showcases the impact of this technology on daily life. The residence is a nationally recognized landmark known for its groundbreaking role in the history of electrification. Constructed in 1882, this Queen Anne–style mansion was the first residence in the US to be illuminated by electricity generated from a central hydroelectric power station. Today, Hearthstone is a museum, preserving its original Edison light fixtures, switches, and wiring.

Appleton's legacy as an electrical pioneer is symbolized by the world's first commercially successful electric street railway. Launched in 1886, the electric streetcar system, propelled by hydroelectric power from the Fox River, was a groundbreaking innovation.

Just as the electric streetcar system served the Appleton area for nearly half a century, another notable figure was finding his footing in the city. Harry Houdini, the world-renowned escape artist, was born in Budapest, Hungary, but he is deeply connected to Appleton. The city became his adopted home when his family immigrated in 1878. Young Ehrich Weiss, later known as Houdini, spent formative years in Appleton, fostering a fascination with magic and illusion that would shape his career. Downtown Houdini Plaza commemorates his legacy, and the History Museum at the Castle houses a dedicated exhibit that explores his life and career.

TIP

Check out This Big One, a massive, over 500-year-old Douglas fir tree in Kaukauna. Originally from Tacoma, Washington, it was moved to its current location by the Army Corps of Engineers.

Eat!

PULLMANS AT TROLLEY SQUARE
619 S Olde Oneida St.

CHARLIE'S DRIVE-IN
806 W Main St., Hortonville

VINCE LOMBARDI'S STEAKHOUSE
333 W College Ave.

Stay!

FRANKLIN STREET INN BED AND BREAKFAST
318 E Franklin St.

Visit!

VULCAN STREET PLANT REPLICA
530 S Vulcan St.

JOHN HART WHORTON HOUSE
315 W Prospect Ave.

THIS BIG ONE
1000-1700 Augustine St.
Kaukauna

LITTLE CHUTE WINDMILL
130 W Main St., Little Chute
920-788-2629

to Do!

THE HISTORY MUSEUM AT THE CASTLE
330 E College Ave.
920-735-9370

HEARTHSTONE HISTORIC HOUSE MUSEUM
625 W Prospect Ave.
920-730-8204

KIMBERLY POINT LIGHTHOUSE
270 Lakeshore Ave., Neenah
920-886-6060

CHARLES A. GRIGNON MANSION
1313 Augustine St., Kaukauna
920-766-6106

ATLAS SCIENCE CENTER
425 W Water St.
920-380-7491

HYDROELECTRIC HERITAGE TRAILWAY
600 S Vulcan St.

FROM APPLETON, head east on US-10 E. Turn right on WI-32/WI-57. Turn right onto Plymouth Street. Turn left onto County Road HH. Turn right onto County Road J. Turn right onto WI-67 S, continuing into Plymouth.

PLYMOUTH

Plymouth has earned its title as the "Cheese Capital of the World" through a rich history deeply intertwined with the dairy industry.

In the late 19th century, with an abundance of milk and a growing population, cheesemaking emerged as a practical way to preserve and utilize surplus dairy. Farmwives often pioneered the art of cheesemaking in their kitchens, creating delicious and long-lasting products for their families.

By the mid-19th century, dedicated cheese factories had begun to appear in Plymouth. One of the earliest was established by Hiram Conover around 1863. The city boasted numerous cheese plants within a few decades, contributing significantly to the local and regional economy.

A pivotal moment in Plymouth's cheese history arrived in 1882 with the establishment of the National Cheese Exchange. This institution played a crucial role in setting the market price for cheddar cheese, solidifying Plymouth's position as a central hub for the dairy industry. The exchange's impact was far-reaching. It attracted cheesemakers, buyers, and traders from across the country, boosting the local economy and enhancing Plymouth's reputation as a cheese epicenter.

Eat!

PJ CAMPBELLS AT THE DEPOT
114 Depot Rd.
920-893-8600

DEO'S PIZZERIA & PUB
417 E Mill St.
920-892-8485

CHESTER'S DRIVE-IN
1504 Eastern Ave.
920-892-7722

MOXIE CAFÉ
301 E Mill St.
920-449-5545

THREE GUYS & A GRILL RESTAURANT
W7039 Co. Rd. S R
Elkhart Lake
920-876-2535

KOEHRING'S GRAND CENTRAL HOUSE
602 Fremont St., Kiel
920-894-7630

ROEPKE'S VILLAGE INN
W2686 St. Charles Rd.
Chilton
920-849-4000

Visit!

ANTOINETTE DAIRY COW STATUE
12 S Milwaukee St.

UNITED STATES POST OFFICE MURAL
(commissioned during FDR's New Deal)
302 E Main St.

HOLY RESURRECTION BYZANTINE CATHOLIC MONASTERY
(make arrangements before visiting)
300 S Second Ave.
St. Nazianz
920-881-4009

TIP

More than just a quirky photo op, the udder-ly delightful *Antionette Dairy Cow* Statue in Plymouth symbolizes the city's dairy history. Erected in 1977 to commemorate Plymouth's centennial, she's a must-see.

Deo's Pizzeria & Pub in Plymouth

Plymouth also gave rise to influential figures in the cheesemaking world. Elmer Eldridge and Harmon Wheeler, both residents of Plymouth, developed innovative cheese-processing methods that advanced the industry as a whole.

Even though the National Cheese Exchange is no longer operational, Plymouth's cheese heritage endures. The city remains home to several major cheese processing facilities, including Sargento, Great Lakes Cheese, Masters Gallery, and Sartori.

to Do!

WESLEY W. JUNG CARRIAGE MUSEUM
W7965 WI-23, Greenbush
920-526-3271

ROAD AMERICA
N7390 WI-67
920-892-4576

CHEESE COUNTER AND DAIRY HERITAGE CENTER
133 E Mill St.
920-892-2012

PINECREST HISTORICAL VILLAGE
924 Pine Crest Ln., Manitowoc
920-684-4445

FROM PLYMOUTH, take WI-67 S. Turn left on County Road E. Turn right on WI-28 S. Turn left onto WI-144 S. Turn left on Cedar Street and right on Main Street in West Bend.

Stay!

ROCHESTER INN
504 Water St.
Sheboygan Falls
866- 467-3122

WEST BEND

A few blocks from Main Street stands a peculiar structure that holds a fascinating window into the past: the Sheriff's Residence and Jail. This historic building, built in 1886, served as the county's law enforcement hub for nearly eight decades before being transformed into an alluring museum. The sheriff's residence was a home for the sheriff and their family, who lived near the inmates. The building's architecture reflects this rare arrangement, with living quarters on one side and the jail cells on the other. In contrast to the sheriff's quarters, thick bars and concrete walls reveal the harsh conditions inmates faced. Explore the lives

Eat!

TIMMER'S RESORT
5151 Timmer Bay Rd.
262-338-7710

THE ORVILLE
518 Poplar St.
262-335-6302

JAIL HOUSE RESTAURANT
897 Pleasant Valley Rd.
262-675-9302

GREAT OUTDOORS SUPPER CLUB
8906 Forest View Rd., Kewaskum
262-334-7977

SAL'S PIZZERIA
161 N Main St.
262-334-3944

BRAZEN HEAD PUB
147 N Main St.
262-334-9750

TIP

At Timmer's Resort, look for the rectangular stone engraved with "TIMMER" in the parking area; it was once a step for buggy-riding guests.

Visit!

REGNER PARK
800 N Main St.
262-335-5080

RIVERFRONT PARKWAY
Roosevelt Dr.

of law enforcers and criminals at the Sheriff's Residence and Jail, part of the Tower Heritage Center.

In contrast to the stark realities at the Sheriff's Residence and Jail, Timmer's Resort on Cedar Lake provides a serene escape. The resort originated in 1863 when Mathias and Margaret Timmer, immigrants from Germany, settled in the area. The Timmer family's legacy took shape in 1882 when they opened their property as a hotel, a venture that would span generations. Guests arriving by buggy and horse-drawn bus, were greeted warmly by Mathias and Margaret's daughter, Mary. The resort's charm and hospitality quickly gained a reputation, drawing visitors from nearby cities like Chicago, St. Louis, and Milwaukee.

Timmer's Resort proved resilient, weathering both Prohibition and the Great Depression. Remarkably, it thrived during Prohibition thanks to a clever beer-smuggling operation via a neighbor's pie delivery truck.

Stay!

CHARLOTTE'S CABIN AT SHALOM WILDLIFE ZOO
1901 Shalom Dr.
262-338-1310

HIDDEN SERENITY BED AND BREAKFAST
1876 Shalom Dr.
262-623-0148

PALOMINO PINES GUEST RANCH
W727 Mill Rd.
Kewaskum
414-307-3430

to Do!

THE TOWER HERITAGE CENTER
320 S Fifth Ave.
262-335-4678

SHERIFF'S RESIDENCE AND JAIL TOUR
320 S Fifth Ave.
262-335-4678

THE BEND THEATER
125 N Main St.
262-346-7156

SHALOM WILDLIFE ZOO
1901 Shalom Dr.
262-338-1310

FROM WEST BEND, take WI-33 E. Turn right on County Road G. Left on County Road NN. Turn right on County Road G. Left on County Road M. Right on Wasaukee Road. Turn left on WI-167. Go south on WI-57 S. Turn right on West Brantwood Avenue in Glendale.

GLENDALE

Solly's Grille, an iconic Glendale institution, has cemented its place in culinary history with its iconic butter burger and a prestigious James Beard Award. Founded in 1936 as Solly's Coffee Shop by Kenneth "Solly" Salmon, the restaurant has been a family-owned and operated staple for generations. Initially located in Milwaukee, Solly's found its permanent home in Glendale in 1971. Known for its classic diner atmosphere and friendly service, Solly's has garnered a loyal following for its signature dish: the butter burger. This creation features a burger cooked on a flattop, steamed in butter, and topped with stewed onions and additional butter, resulting in a rich and indulgent flavor that has become a Wisconsin culinary staple.

Solly's Grille, home of The Butter Burger since 1936

In 2022, Solly's Grille achieved a major milestone by winning the James Beard Foundation's America's Classics Award. This esteemed recognition honors locally owned restaurants with timeless appeal and beloved regional status. The award solidified Solly's place as a culinary treasure and a must-visit destination for food lovers nationwide.

The Fieber family has owned and operated Solly's since its inception, maintaining the restaurant's character and commitment to quality. From its humble beginnings as a coffee shop to its current status as an award-winning restaurant, Solly's Grille continues to delight customers.

Eat!

SOLLY'S GRILLE
4629 N Port Washington Rd.
414-332-8808

THE BAVARIAN BIERHAUS
700 W Lexington Blvd.
414-236-7000

KOPP'S FROZEN CUSTARD
5373 N Port Washington Rd.
414-961-3288

JACK PANDL'S WHITEFISH BAY INN
1319 E Henry Clay St.
Whitefish Bay
414-964-3800

BUTTERMINT
4195 N Oakland Ave.
Shorewood
414-488-2587

THREE LIONS PUB
4515 N Oakland Ave.
Shorewood
414-763-6992

THE LANDMARK INN
10634 W Freistadt Rd.
Mequon
262-242-9907

HUBBARD PARK LODGE
3565 N Morris Blvd.
Shorewood
414-332-4207

Visit!

SCHLITZ AUDUBON NATURE CENTER
1111 E Brown Deer Rd.
Bayside

HISTORIC MILWAUKEE TOWN HALL
5909 N Milwaukee River Pkwy.
414-228-1700

OLDEST LUTHERAN CHURCH IN WISCONSIN
10729 W Freistadt Rd.
Mequon

TRINITY FREISTADT HISTORICAL SITE PICNIC SHELTER
11823 N Church Pl.
Mequon

BENJAMIN CHURCH HOUSE
(Kilbourntown House)
4250 Estabrook Pkwy.
Shorewood
414-273-8288

KLETZSCH PARK
6560 N Milwaukee River Pkwy.
414-461-0839

to Do!

MILWAUKEE POLICE HISTORICAL SOCIETY
6680 N Teutonia Ave.
Milwaukee
414-935-7960

TIP

Don't miss the chance to climb the Schlitz Audubon Nature Center's Observation Tower, built in 1986. The tower offers stunning panoramic views of Lake Michigan and the surrounding natural beauty.

Even the cows line up for Kopp's Frozen Custard.

LAKE SUPERIOR
MINNESOTA
DULUTH
SUPERIOR
APOSTLE ISLANDS
WASHBURN
ASHLAND
IRONWOOD
CHEQUAMEGON NATIONAL FOREST
LAND O' LAKES
EAGLE RIVER
NICOLET NATIONAL FOREST
DANBURY
HAYWARD
PARK FALLS
SPOONER
PHILLIPS
RHINELANDER
CAMERON
LADYSMITH
ST CROIX FALLS
MERRILL
NEW RICHMOND
MEDFORD
ANTIGO
NEAPOLIS
ST PAUL
HUDSON
CHIPPEWA FALLS
WISCONSIN
MENOMONIE
EAU CLAIRE
PRESCOTT
SHAWA
MARSHFIELD
CLINTONV
STOCKHOLM
MONDOVI
NEILLSVILLE
STEVENS POINT
WISCONSIN RAPIDS
WAUPACA
WHITEHALL
ALMA
BLACK RIVER FALLS
PETENWELL DAM
MISSISSIPPI RIVER
WAUTOMA
TOMAH
CASTLE ROCK LAKE
LA CROSSE
NEW LISBON
WESTBY
PORTAGE
BEA DAM
RICHLAND CENTER
IOWA
LAKE MENDOTA
BOSCOBEL
MADISON
STOUGHTON
DODGEVILLE
LANCASTER
JANESVILLE
MONROE
DUBUQUE
ILLINOIS

THE YELLOWSTONE TRAIL AND THE GREAT RIVER ROAD

Beginning in Eau Claire and ending in Alma, this road trip travels through towns that lumber barons helped build, rolling hills and deep valleys in the Driftless Region, and historic roads.

The influx of European settlers led to booming logging camps, sawmills, and agricultural communities. The 19th century marked the heyday of the lumber industry in the Chippewa Valley. Vast forests of white pine were harvested, fueling the economy and attracting thousands of workers. Lumber barons built grand mansions, and bustling towns supported the industry.

Scandinavian immigrants played a significant role in shaping the region. Their influence can be seen in Eau Claire's Norwegian ski jumping culture and near the Mississippi River in the profoundly traditional Swedish small town of Stockholm.

The Yellowstone Trail, a historic automobile route spanning the United States, passed through Northwest Wisconsin. This pioneering trail, established in 1912, played a vital role in the early days of automobile travel, connecting communities across the country. The trail's route through Eau Claire, Chippewa Falls, Menomonie, and Hudson followed the main streets, allowing visitors to experience the towns' downtown areas. Tranquil two-lane roads connect the Yellowstone Trail and the Great River Road between Hudson and Prescott. However, the Great River Road National Scenic Byway is Wisconsin's only National Scenic Byway. This route lazily meanders beside the Mississippi River from Prescott to Alma.

TO START THE TOUR, **DOWNTOWN EAU CLAIRE** at the Local Store and drive west ending alongside the Mississippi River in Alma.

EAU CLAIRE

After the Civil War, lumber barons built over 30 sawmills that lined the banks of the Eau Claire and Chippewa Rivers. Eau Claire had more lumber mills than anywhere in the world, and by 1890 over 75 sawmills and factories made and shipped wood products nationwide. Eau Claire, with its abundance of forests, combined with the confluence of the rivers, an oxbow lake, and natural inlets to hold logs, became known as Sawdust City.

Perhaps Eau Claire's "Indie Music Capital of the Midwest" title stemmed from its early logging camps. In the 1890s, six out of 10 lumberjacks immigrated from Northern Europe. Music became the universal language, and rousing Saturday night entertainment allowed music to bypass the limitations of words. In the 1950s and '60s, Eau Claire became a Midwest hotbed for significant rock and roll and jazz performers—mostly because of the groundwork laid by the University of Wisconsin-Eau Claire jazz program. Musicians found a welcoming city for performances in backrooms and ballrooms.

To experience what makes Eau Claire tick, visit Carson Park and its many historical attractions, namely the Paul Bunyan Logging Camp and the Chippewa Valley Museum. Go to the Joynt, where many of America's jazz greats played in the back unbeknownst to the public. Eat at Sammy's Pizza, although in a different location; Buddy Holly, Ritchie Valens, and the Big Bopper ate at this Pizza Hall of Fame restaurant after their concert on January 26, 1959—days before their fatal plane crash while on the Winter Dance Party tour.

One of the few places in America to watch Ski Jumping
Courtesy of Tim Manus

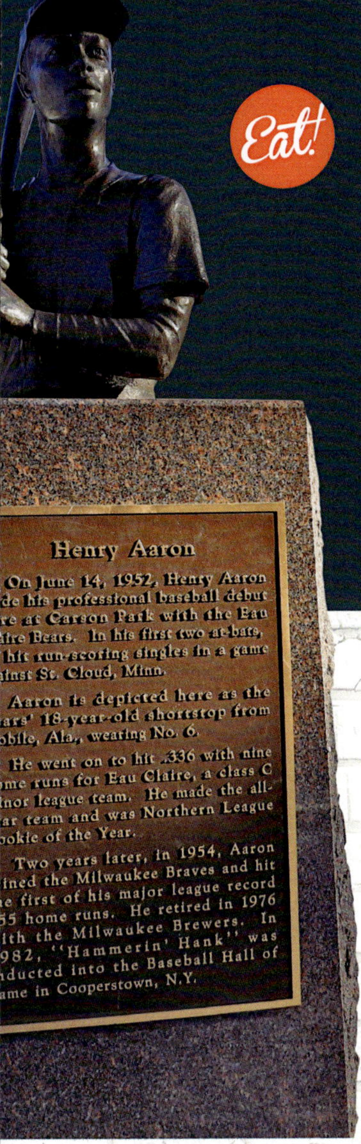

Henry "Hammerin' Hank" Aaron statue in Carson Park

Eat!

THE LIVERY RESTAURANT & SALOON
316 Wisconsin St.
715-833-7666

RAY'S PLACE
838 Water St.
715-832-3991

SAMMY'S PIZZA RESTAURANT & PUB
2812 London Rd.
715-831-1300

VALLEY BURGER COMPANY
1004 Menomonie St.
715-514-0498

NORSKE NOOK
13804 W Seventh St.
Osseo
715-597-3069

TIP

Experience Eau Claire's Norwegian heritage through its thrilling ski jumping tradition. The city boasts two world-class jumps: the Flying Eagles Ski Club, featuring a 55-meter hill, and the 90-meter Silver Mine Ski Jump.

Visit!

BIG FALLS COUNTY PARK
600 Big Falls Forest Rd.
715-839-4783

JAMES NEWMAN CLARK BIRD MUSEUM
101 Roosevelt Ave.
715-836-4166

Stay!

THE OXBOW HOTEL
516 Galloway St.
715-839-0601

FROM DOWNTOWN EAU CLAIRE, take Main Street, then go north on US-53. After crossing the Chippewa River, turn right onto West River Street. You will arrive downtown at the North Bridge Street roundabout.

to Do!

MT. WASHINGTON NORDIC SKI COMPLEX
1805 W Menomonie St.

AGER HOUSE AND THE CENTER FOR NORDIC CULTURE
514 W Madison St.
715-834-5204

CARSON PARK
100 Carson Park Dr.
715-839-5039

BANBURY PLACE MARKETS AND HISTORY TOUR
930 Galloway St.
Building 13, Ste. 29
715-834-6624

THE LOCAL STORE
205 N Dewey St.
715-552-0457

LAZY MONK BREWING
97 W Madison St.
715-271-0848

REVIVAL RECORDS
128 S Barstow St.
715-514-4202

CHIPPEWA FALLS

Chippewa Falls owes much of its historical significance to two titans of industry: lumber and beer. The city's strategic location on the Chippewa River, a vital waterway for timber transportation, propelled it to the forefront of the nation's lumber industry in the late 19th century. Simultaneously, the booming brewery scene, exemplified by Leinenkugel's, thrived on the demand created by the lumberjacks and mill workers.

For a brief period, Chippewa Falls was home to the world's largest lumber mill. The economic impact of this lumber giant was immense. It fueled the growth of Chippewa Falls, attracting businesses and residents alike. The city's infrastructure expanded rapidly to accommodate the influx of workers and their families. However, the industry was unsustainable. As the forests dwindled, so too did the lumber mill's fortunes. Its closure marked the end of an era, but the city's legacy as a lumber town would endure.

While the lumber industry was reaching its zenith, another enterprise took root in Chippewa Falls. In 1867, a German immigrant, Jacob Leinenkugel, established a brewery that would become synonymous with the city. The abundant, pure water from the Chippewa River provided the ideal conditions for brewing, and the thirsty lumberjacks and mill workers created a ready market for Leinenkugel's beer. As the lumber industry declined, Leinenkugel's continued to grow. Today, Leinenkugel's brewery is a popular tourist destination, offering tours, tastings, and a glimpse into the rich history of this iconic Wisconsin company.

Jacob Leinenkugel Brewing Company

Chippewa Candy Shop

TIP

A tour of the Jacob Leinenkugel Brewing Company is a journey through time and flavor. Discover the Leinenkugel family's brewing legacy as you explore the historic brewery.

Stay!

INN ON LAKE WISSOTA
16649 96th Ave.
715-382-4401

MCLAREN HOUSE BED & BREAKFAST
522 Superior St.
715-720-7367

Eat!

SHEELEY HOUSE SALOON
236 W River St.
715-723-4331

MAX'S BISTRO & BAR
213 N Bridge St.
715-861-2500

BRESINA'S CARRY OUT
10 Jefferson Ave.
715-723-7869

WISSOTA HIGH SHORES SUPPER CLUB
17985 Co. Hwy. X
715-215-2981

ANDERSON'S CHIC-N-FISH
615 W Park Ave.
715-861-3911

DYLAN'S DAIRY
120 Main St., Cornell
715-239-6997

to Do!

JACOB LEINENKUGEL BREWING COMPANY & TOUR
124 E Elm St.
888-534-6437

IRVINE PARK ZOO
125 Bridgewater Ave.
715-723-0051

CHIPPEWA FALLS MUSEUM OF INDUSTRY & TECHNOLOGY
21 E Grand Ave.
715-720-9206

COOK RUTLEDGE MANSION
505 W Grand Ave.
715-723-7181

VISITORS CENTER & RAIL MUSEUM
205 W Ninth St. S
Ladysmith
715-532-2642

Visit!

BRUNET ISLAND STATE PARK
23125 255th St.
Cornell
715-239-6888

RECLAIMED FLAMBEAU MINE
WI-27 and
Blackberry Lane
Ladysmith

LEAVING CHIPPEWA FALLS, head west on County Road N. Take a left on WI-40. In Colfax, take a right on WI-170 W. In Wheeler, take a left on WI-25 S. Continue into Menomonie.

MENOMONIE

The Mabel Tainter Center for the Arts is an ornate Victorian-era building that was originally conceived as a memorial to Mabel Tainter, a young woman who died tragically.

Built in 1889 by Mabel's parents, Captain and Mrs. Andrew Tainter, the building was initially named the Mabel Tainter Memorial Building. Thanks to their involvement in the lumber industry, it was a period of immense wealth for the Tainter family. The decision to create this grand structure as a tribute to their daughter was in honor of their love and loss.

Designed by architect Harvey Ellis, the Mabel Tainter is a stunning example of Romanesque architecture. The building's impressive exterior is composed of Dunnville sandstone, sourced from the Red Cedar River near Downsville, while the interior is an opulent showcase of Victorian craftsmanship. Intricate hand-stenciling, hand-carved white pine archways, leaded glass windows, and gleaming brass fixtures adorn the space, creating an atmosphere of timeless elegance.

In the 1970s, a dedicated group of community members recognized the building's historical and architectural significance. With their efforts, the Mabel Tainter was restored to its former glory and reopened as a performing arts center.

Today, the building also houses art exhibits, workshops, and community events, fostering a vibrant arts scene in Menomonie. Moreover, the facility has earned widespread recognition for its historical significance. The facility is listed on the National Register of Historic Places and has been designated a Wisconsin Historical Marker Site. It is also a charter member of the League of Historic American Theatres.

See one of the world's largest public displays of dining car china at the Colfax Railroad Museum.

Find candy and treats from around the world at C & J's Candy Store. Courtesy of Tim Manus

Eat!

JAKE'S SUPPER CLUB
E5690 Co. Rd. D
715-235-2465

SCATTERBRAIN CAFÉ
E4507 Co. Rd. C
715-664-8260

THE STONE BARN
S685 Co. Rd. KK
Nelson
715-673-4478

CORRAL BAR & RIVERSIDE GRILL
318 W Main St.
Durand
715-672-8874

VINO CAPPUCCINO ARTISAN BISTRO
N5734 US-12
Elk Mound
715-879-4157

A LITTLE SLICE OF ITALY
501 Main St., Colfax
715-962-4444

to Do!

HISTORIC MABEL TAINTER CENTER FOR THE ARTS
205 Main St. E
715-235-0001

WILSON PLACE MANSION
101 Wilson Ct.
715-235-2283

C & J's CANDY STORE & SCOOP SHOPPE
342 Main St. E
715-308-7732

COLFAX RAILROAD MUSEUM
500 E Railroad Ave.
Colfax
715-962-2076

CHIPPEWA VALLEY MOTOR CAR ASSOCIATION
S89 WI-25, Durand

ELK MOUND HILL CASTLE
Elk Mound Hill Road, Elk Mound
715-879-5011

CRYSTAL CAVE
W965 WI-29
Spring Valley
715-778-4414

TIP

Step back in time with C&J's Candy Store & Scoop Shoppe's collection of retro and vintage candies, or embark on a global flavor adventure with goodies from over 60 countries.

Stay!

OAKLAWN INN
423 Technology Dr. E
715-235-6155

Visit!

DEVIL'S PUNCHBOWL PRESERVE
410th St.
715-235-8850

FOLLOW BROADWAY STREET SOUTH and turn right on WI-29 W. In River Falls, turn right onto WI-35/WI-65 N. Keep left to continue on WI-35 N. Use the left lane to take the I-94 W N exit toward Hudson. Take exit 1 for Hudson.

HUDSON

Hudson sits on the historic Yellowstone Trail, a pioneering transcontinental route that carved its path through the heart of America. Established in 1912, the Yellowstone Trail was a visionary project aimed at creating a continuous, well-maintained road from Plymouth Rock, Massachusetts, to Puget Sound, Washington.

Before the era of numbered highways, the Yellowstone Trail was a beacon for intrepid motorists seeking adventure and exploration. Its passage through Wisconsin, including the city of Hudson, affirmed the burgeoning automobile culture and the growing desire for long-distance travel. The trail's impact on Hudson was profound. It contributed to the city's economic growth and development, attracting travelers and businesses alike.

TIP

Wisconsin's pioneering numbered highway system in 1918 contributed to the influx of travelers, including those on the Yellowstone Trail, influencing the development of Hudson's downtown buildings.

Dine along the river in Hudson.

Though the original roadbed has been transformed over the years, there are still opportunities to connect with the spirit of this historic route. Yellowstone Trail Heritage Day is an annual event celebrating Hudson's rich history and heritage and its role in the nation's first transcontinental road. This celebration brings together history buffs, car enthusiasts, and families for a day of fun, education, and nostalgia. Held each August, the event showcases the significance of the Yellowstone Trail in shaping the region's development. Visitors can explore the trail's history through exhibits, guided tours, and historical reenactments. Vintage vehicle displays are a highlight, showcasing the types of cars that traversed the trail in its heyday.

to Do!

KINNI CREEK LODGE AND OUTFITTERS
545 N Main St., River Falls
715-425-7378

ST. CROIX RIVER CRUISES
98 Walnut St.
651-436-8883

OCTAGON HOUSE MUSEUM
1004 Third St.
715-386-2654

BASS LAKE CHEESE FACTORY
598 Valley View Trail, Somerset
715-247-5585

SWINGING BRIDGE BREWING COMPANY
122 S Main St., River Falls
715-629-1464

GREAT RIVER ROAD VISITOR AND LEARNING CENTER
200 Monroe St., Prescott
715-262-0104

Visit!

WILLOW RIVER STATE PARK
1034 Co. Hwy. A
715-386-5931

Eat!

BLACK ROOSTER BISTRO
516 Second St.
715-808-0560

POST AMERICAN EATERY
225 Locust St.
715-377-4699

BARKER'S BAR & GRILL
413 Second St.
715-386-4123

PIER 500
500 First St.
715-386-5504

THE KITCHEN TABLE
211 Broad St., Prescott
715-262-2223

Stay!

RIVER'S EDGE APPLE RIVER TUBING & CAMPING
1820 Raleigh Rd.
New Richmond
715-247-3305

KINNI CREEK LODGE AND OUTFITTERS
545 N Main St., River Falls
715-425-7378

FROM HUDSON, travel south on WI-35 S. At the traffic circle, take the second exit onto WI-65 S. Turn right on County Road O. Turn left onto US-10 E. Turn right onto US-63 S. Turn left onto WI-35/Great River Road.

STOCKHOLM

Stockholm, a small town of 82 residents, proudly preserves its Swedish heritage. In the mid-19th century, Swedish pioneers, led by visionary adventurer Erik Petterson, sought new opportunities along the Mississippi River. In 1851, Petterson climbed the bluff overlooking Lake Pepin and declared it the ideal location for a settlement. The town's name honors the founders' Swedish roots, a nod to their homeland's capital city.

Swedish immigrants poured into the area, seeking refuge from poverty and hardship. They brought their language, customs, and traditions, which quickly took root in the new land. The town flourished, becoming a vital hub for Scandinavian immigrants heading westward.

Stockholm evolved from a Scandinavian settlement into an agricultural center. In 1880, its population peaked at 280 residents, supported by essential businesses like general stores, hardware shops, and blacksmiths. The railroad's arrival in 1886 further solidified Stockholm's connection to regional markets.

Eat!

HUMBLE MOON FOLKSTEAD AND SALOON
W12128 WI-35
715-495-0743

HAGER HEIGHTS DRIVE-IN
7866 170th Ave.
Hager City
715-792-2118

CHEF SHACK BAY CITY
W6379 Main St., Bay City
715-594-3060

SMILING PELICAN BAKE SHOP
W3556 WI-35
Maiden Rock
715-448-3807

HARBOR VIEW CAFÉ
314 First St., Pepin
715-442-3893

J & J BBQ & CATERING
208 N Main St., Nelson
715-673-4717

Stay!

MAIDEN ROCK INN
N531 Co. Rd. S
Maiden Rock
715-448-2608

PEPIN FARM POTTERY AND GUESTHOUSE
3706 110th Ave.
Maiden Rock
715-448-3300

HARBOR HILL INN
310 Second St., Pepin
715-600-2466

to Do!

STOCKHOLM PIE AND GENERAL STORE
N2030 Spring St.
715-442-5505

VILLA BELLEZZA WINERY & VINEYARDS
1420 Third St., Pepin
715-442-2424

LAURA INGALLS WILDER MUSEUM
306 Third St., Pepin
715-513-9115

SWEDISH HISTORY MUSEUM
2030 Spring St.

NELSON CREAMERY
S237 WI-35, Nelson
715-673-4725

Swedish History Museum in the old post office

TIP

The Stockholm Pie and General Store is more than just legendary pies; it's a favorite Wisconsin experience. Don't miss the delicious sandwiches and locally sourced goods.

Stockholm adapted to the post–World War I rural exodus by focusing on grain warehousing, clamming, commercial fishing, ice harvesting, and farm machinery sales. The similar post–World War II exodus to cities and the loss of the railroad threatened Stockholm's survival. Yet the town's charm proved enduring. Beginning in the 1970s, artists and urban dwellers rediscovered Stockholm, revitalizing its historic buildings and cultivating a robust cultural scene. A new wave of entrepreneurs followed, recognizing the town's potential for a second-to-none blend of Swedish heritage, natural beauty, and artistic expression.

FROM STOCKHOLM, take WI-35 S/Great River Road along the river to Alma.

Visit!

LITTLE HOUSE WAYSIDE CABIN
N3238 Co. Rd. CC
715-513-6383

ALMA

Alma owes its existence to the Mississippi River. The town's history is deeply intertwined with the river's flow, shaping its development from a frontier outpost to a thriving community. Originally inhabited by Native Americans, the area's transformation began in the mid-19th century when European settlers arrived. The river, with its abundant resources and transportation capabilities, became the lifeblood of the community. Sawmills, grist mills, and other industries sprang up along its banks, fueling the town's growth.

The arrival of steamboats further solidified Alma's status as a river town. These majestic vessels brought goods and people to the area, contributing to its economic prosperity. The town's architecture reflects its riverfront heritage, with many historical buildings showcasing the charm of a bygone era.

This ambiance extends to Alma's accommodations, which blend history and modern comfort. Three establishments that capture the town's essence along the Mississippi River are the Hotel de Ville, the Alma Hotel, and the Blue Door Inn. The Hotel de Ville is a southern French-inspired property with a collection of historic buildings, each with its distinct character. The Blue Door Inn's 19th-century structure provides a classic experience, while the Alma Hotel blends its time-honored ambiance and contemporary conveniences. The Alma Hotel café serves a nostalgic experience with its vintage counter, stools, and local memorabilia displayed against a checkered floor.

Inside the Castlerock Museum

Eat!

ALFRESCO PIZZERIA
211 N Main St.
608-685-3340

ALMA BAKERY
105 Main St.
608-418-9945

ALMA HOTEL, BAR & CAFÉ
201 N Main St.
608-685-3380

Visit!

THE GYPSY WAGON CURIOSITY SHOP
305 N Main St.
612- 423-3653

PRAIRIE MOON SCULPTURE GARDENS
52727 Prairie Moon Rd.
Fountain City
608-687-8250

BUENA VISTA PARK
Buena Vista Rd.

Stay!

HOTEL DE VILLE
305 N Main St.
612- 423-3653

THE BURLINGTON HOTEL & BAR
809 N Main St.
612- 207-2826

BLUE DOOR INN ALMA
331 S Main St.
608-685-9700

THE TRITSCH HOUSE
601 S Second St.
507-450-6573

to Do!

CASTLEROCK MUSEUM
402 S Second St.
608-685-4231

BIG RIVER THEATRE
121 Main St.
612- 751-1970

WINGS OVER ALMA
110 N Main St.
608-685-3303

THE COMMERCIAL
7715, 305 S Main St.
608-418-0144

ELMER'S AUTO & TOY MUSEUM
W903 Elmers Rd.
Fountain City

TIP

Take advantage of the breathtaking panoramic views of the Mississippi River from Buena Vista Park's overlook above Alma. Watch as the sky explodes with color from sunsets.

Buena Vista Park

LAKE SUPERIOR
NNESOTA
DULUTH
SUPERIOR
WASHBURN
ASHLAND
APOSTLE ISLANDS
IRONWOOD
CHEQUAMEGON NATIONAL FOREST
DANBURY
HAYWARD
PARK FALLS
SPOONER
LAND O' LAKES
EAGLE RIVER
NICOLET NATIONAL FOREST
KINSFORD
PHILLIPS
RHINELANDER
CAMERON
LADYSMITH
ROIX LS
MEDFORD
MERRILL
ANTIGO
W RICHMOND
WISCONSIN
CHIPPEWA FALLS
MENOMONIE
EAU CLAIRE
OCONTO FALLS
SHAWANO
MARSHFIELD
CLINTONVILLE
MONDOVI
NEILLSVILLE
STEVENS POINT
WHITEHALL
WISCONSIN RAPIDS
WAUPACA
BLACK RIVER FALLS
PETENWELL DAM
MISSISSIPPI RIVER
WAUTOMA
TOMAH
SPARTA
CASTLE ROCK LAKE
LA CROSSE
NEW LISBON
LAKE WINNEBAGO
SHEBO
WESTBY
PORTAGE
BEAVER DAM
WEST BEND
VIROQUA
RICHLAND CENTER
IOWA
MENOMONEE FALLS
LAKE MENDOTA
BOSCOBEL
MADISON
PRAIRIE DU CHIEN
MILWAUKEE
DODGEVILLE
STOUGHTON
LANCASTER
PLATTEVILLE
JANESVILLE
MONROE
DUBUQUE
ILLINOIS
MIC
61
26
13
2
45
28
77
53
63
51
141
35
70
27
8
32
64
94
10
39
49
29
37
90
57
23
82
58
41
151
14
16
18
12
43
78
11

THE GREAT RIVER ROAD AND DRIFTLESS REGION

The Great River Road, a scenic byway stretching along the Mississippi River, offers a journey through Wisconsin's rich history and stunning landscapes. The Driftless Region, a unique geological area untouched by the glaciers that shaped much of the Midwest, provides a backdrop of rolling hills, fertile valleys, and meandering rivers.

The Mississippi River played a vital role in the fur trade, and many towns along the Great River Road have a connection to this era. Prairie du Chien was pivotal when French explorers established a trading post in the 17th century. Visit historic sites and museums to learn about the fur trading industry and the Native American tribes who inhabited the region.

Wisconsin's Great River Road region also has a deep immigrant history, with waves of settlers arriving from Europe and beyond by steamboats and railroads. The region's architecture, cuisine, and festivals show its diverse cultural heritage. In Westby, the Snowflake Ski Club holds world-class ski jumping events that Norwegian immigrants initially organized. Norwegian immigrants also thrived in tobacco farming. Now, several remaining tobacco warehouses hold businesses in Viroqua.

As the lumber industry deteriorated, German immigrants relied on their brewing traditions to rapidly expand their production. Their expertise led to a thriving craft beer scene. Today, breweries like Potosi Brewing Company offer a diverse selection of handcrafted brews. Explore the National Brewing Museum in Potosi and get a photograph of the Heileman's Old Style World's Largest Six-Pack in La Crosse.

TO START THE TOUR, THE INTERNATIONAL FRIENDSHIP GARDENS in La Crosse and drive alongside the Mississippi River before ending the loop in Sparta.

LA CROSSE

La Crosse's strategic position at the Mississippi and Black rivers' confluence made it an ideal fur trading hub. In 1841, the first trading post was established where Riverside Park is located alongside the Mississippi River.

During the mid-1800s, steamboats brought thousands of settlers, many of which were immigrants, to towns on both sides of the Mississippi River. As America grew, so did the need for lumber. La Crosse and its surrounding area, known as the Coulee Region, had abundant forests of white pine that supplied America's rapid expansion during the late 19th century. Logging and sawmill jobs brought European immigrants to La Crosse, with many arriving on the paddlewheels. Steamboat transportation climaxed in 1857 with 1,569 dockings, the most of any northern Mississippi River city. As more railroads were built, the need for steamboats eventually faded out. By 1892, the city's population had swelled to over 25,000 people.

TIP

The Dahl Auto Museum showcases automobile history, focusing on the Ford Motor Company and restored classic cars from the early 20th century to the present.

Sunny the Sunfish

European immigrants turned to brewing beer, making La Crosse a leading city that rivaled the nation's best brewing cities, such as Milwaukee. Heileman Brewing Company became the fourth-largest American brewery after Prohibition. Heileman's famous and nostalgic brand, Old Style, sponsored the Chicago Cubs from the 1950s through 2013.

To experience La Crosse, take a paddlewheel cruise on the La Crosse Queen and eat at the Freighthouse Restaurant, a historic railroad lover's dream. Stay at the Charmant Hotel, built in 1898 and previously an iconic candy factory, or at the beautifully restored Lumber Baron Inn.

Eat!

THE FREIGHTHOUSE RESTAURANT
107 Vine St.
608-784-6211

THE PEARL ICE CREAM PARLOR
207 Pearl St.
608-782-6655

THE SWEET SHOP
1113 Caledonia St.
608-784-7724

RIVOLI THEATRE AND PIZZERIA
117 Fourth St. N
608-860-0983

RUDY'S DRIVE-IN RESTAURANT
1004 La Crosse St.
608-782-2200

Visit!

WORLD'S LARGEST SIX-PACK
1106 Third St. S

SUNNY THE SUNFISH
701 Second Ave. N
Onalaska

RIVERSIDE PARK AND INTERNATIONAL FRIENDSHIP GARDENS
100 State St.
608-789-7533

GRANDAD BLUFF PARK
3020 Grandad Bluff Rd.
608-789-7533

to Do!

LA CROSSE QUEEN CRUISES
405 E Veterans Memorial Dr.
608-784-8523

DAHL AUTO MUSEUM
711 Third St. S
608-791-6494

SHRINE OF OUR LADY OF GUADALUPE
(tour and rosary walk)
5250 Justin Rd.
608-799-4059

HISTORIC TROLLEY TOURS
123 Seventh St. S
608-782-2366

World's Largest Six-Pack

Stay!

THE CHARMANT HOTEL
101 State St.
608-519-8800

LUMBER BARON INN
421 Second Ave. N
Onalaska
608-781-8938

FROM LACROSSE, take WI-35 S along the Mississippi River to Prairie Du Chien.

PRAIRIE DU CHIEN

Prairie du Chien's location at the Mississippi and Wisconsin rivers' confluence made it a vital hub for Native American tribes and, later, European explorers. French fur traders established a presence in the 17th century, recognizing the area's potential as a trading post.

The region became a battleground during the French and Indian War and the War of 1812, with Fort Crawford playing a crucial role after that. The fort's subsequent rebuilding solidified Prairie du Chien's importance as a military outpost. Soon after, Black Hawk, a Sauk leader, fought to reclaim ancestral lands lost to white settlers. His resistance culminated in the Black Hawk War of 1832. Ultimately outnumbered and outgunned, Black Hawk surrendered to US forces at Prairie du Chien.

As the city's original site, St. Feriole Island Park is steeped in local lore. Once a bustling fur-trading center, the island's history is etched into its very soil. Buildings like the Brisbois Store, a stone structure dating back to the 1850s, give a glimpse into the era. Similarly, Villa Louis, a magnificent Victorian mansion on the banks of the Mississippi River, provides a captivating window into Prairie du Chien's history. Built by the Dousman family, descendants of a prominent fur trader, the estate reflects the luxury of the 19th century. Visitors can explore the meticulously restored interior, admire the stunning river views, and learn about the Dousman family's significant role in shaping the region.

Eat!

PETE'S HAMBURGER STAND
118 W Blackhawk Ave.
608-326-2635

WINNESHIEK BAR & GRILL
32785 Co. Rd. K
608-326-1068

GREAT RIVER ROADHOUSE
9660 WI-35, De Soto
608-648-2045

FORT MULLIGAN'S GRILLPUB
214 W Blackhawk Ave.
608-326-0639

MUDDY WATERS PIZZA PUB
207 W Blackhawk Ave.
608-380-1283

SPRING LAKE INN
64040 Co. Rd. N
Eastman
608-326-1882

Stay!

COULEE JUNCTION CABOOSE
10414 Coulee Creek Rd.
Ferryville
608-381-6498

GRANDVIEW MOTEL
14812 WI-35, Ferryville
608-734-3235

LATARNIA GUEST HOUSE
58965 Lucky Ln.
Eastman
630-418-5685

Visit!

ST. FERIOLE ISLAND PARK
101 N Fourth St.
608-326-6406

FORT CRAWFORD MUSEUM
717 S Beaumont Rd.
608-326-6960

WYALUSING STATE PARK
13081 State Park Ln.
Bagley
608-996-2261

to Do!

MAIDEN VOYAGE TOURS
101 Water St., Marquette, IA
563-586-2123

GREAT RIVER ROAD INTERPRETIVE CENTER
S5524 WI-35, Genoa
608-689-2605

VALLEY FISH & CHEESE
304 S Prairie St.
608-326-4719

TIP

Visit the Cannery gift shop. Constructed in 1912 as the Prairie du Chien City Canning Company, this 30,000-square-foot facility once canned local produce, particularly sauerkraut and tomatoes.

The Dousman House at Villa Louis historic site

LEAVING PRAIRIE DU CHIEN, take US-18/Great River Road East. Turn right on County Highway K. Turn left on US-61. Exit right on bypass US-61/129 and continue south. Turn left on WI-81/61/35. At the traffic circle, go left on WI-81 and follow it into Platteville.

PLATTEVILLE

Platteville's history is connected with the discovery of lead ore in the early 19th century. The influx of miners and settlers transformed the area from a wilderness into a bustling mining town.

At the Mining and Rollo Jamison Museums, you can explore an authentic 1845 lead mine, ride a historic mine train, and discover the fascinating Jamison collection of local artifacts. The museums offer a comprehensive look at the region's past.

Nearby, the Potosi Brewing Company boasts a storied past. Founded in 1852, it thrived for decades, becoming a Wisconsin brewing giant. Despite closing in 1972, the brewery's legacy endured. Thanks to community efforts, it reopened in 2008 after extensive restoration.

The National Brewery Museum, housed within the historic Potosi Brewing Company, features a vast collection of beer-related artifacts, from bottles and cans to advertising memorabilia. The museum offers a fascinating journey through brewing history.

The Mining & Rollo Jamison Museums

While beer enthusiasts will enjoy exploring the National Brewery Museum, the First Capitol Historic Site in Belmont, Wisconsin, is a fascinating glimpse into the state's early history. The preserved complex houses two original buildings in which Wisconsin's first legislative session convened in 1836. Visitors can step back in time and explore the rooms where the foundation of Wisconsin's government was laid. The site offers a unique opportunity to appreciate the challenges and triumphs of the territory's early settlers.

TIP

The historic Sinsinawa Dominican Sisters campus tour includes the Queen of the Rosary Chapel, with its stunning stained-glass windows, and the Mound, a sacred Native American site.

Eat!

OWL CAFÉ
80 N Second St.
608-348-4416

BEASTRO SE7EN
45 N Second St.
608-348-2798

THE LEMON DOOR
1030 Lincoln Ave.
Fennimore
608-822-0002

UDDER BROTHERS' CREAMERY & RESTAURANT
1100 Elm St., Boscobel
608-391-3120

Visit!

MITCHELL-ROUNTREE STONE COTTAGE
460 W Madison St.
608-723-4925

FIRST CAPITOL HISTORIC SITE
18904 Co. Rd. G, Belmont
608-987-2122

SINSINAWA DOMINICAN SISTERS
585 Co. Rd. Z, Sinsinawa
608-748-4411

STONEFIELD HISTORIC SITE
12195 Co. Hwy. VV
Cassville
608-725-5210

DICKEYVILLE GROTTO & SHRINES
255-377 Great River Rd.
Dickeyville
608-568-3119

ST. AUGUSTINE CHURCH
Hill St. (located in New Diggings), Shullsburg

to Do!

THE MINING & ROLLO JAMISON MUSEUMS
405 E Main St.
608-348-3301

POTOSI BREWERY AND ABA NATIONAL BREWERY MUSEUM
209 S Main St., Potosi
608-763-4002

CARR VALLEY CHEESE CO.
675 Lincoln Ave.
Fennimore
608-820-8818

Stay!

THE FENWAY HOUSE HOTEL
1096 Lincoln Ave.
Fennimore
608-822-3782

UPPER MISSISSIPPI RIVER LODGING
105 W Amelia St.
Cassville
608-723-8807

FROM PLATTEVILLE, take US-61 North. Turn left onto US-14W/US-61. At the traffic circle, take the second exit and stay on US-14 W/US-61 N. Exit the traffic circle onto US-14 W/US-61 N. Continue into Viroqua.

TIP

Be sure to visit Driftless Books and Music, located in an old tobacco warehouse. It's believed to have over one million unique and hard-to-find used books.

Downtown Viroqua

VIROQUA

In the heart of Wisconsin's Driftless Region, tobacco was once a cornerstone of Viroqua's economy. Immigrant farmers, particularly Norwegians, introduced tobacco farming to the region in the late 19th century. While tobacco farming has declined significantly, the historic warehouses remain as reminders of this critical chapter in Viroqua's history. For example, the Viroqua Warehouse was a vital hub for local farmers. As the tobacco industry evolved, the warehouse adapted, undergoing various transformations. This historic structure has been revitalized into a dynamic space, combining its storied past with modern amenities, offering a blend of history and contemporary living.

Viroqua's commitment to sustainability and organic living has deep roots. The region's agricultural heritage and a growing awareness of environmental concerns fostered a fertile ground for this movement. In the 1960s and 1970s, a counterculture spirit began to take hold, leading to increased interest in natural foods and sustainable practices.

While the counterculture movement shaped Viroqua's present, the city's history is marked by earlier pivotal moments. On July 4, 1856, Lucy Stone, a prominent women's rights and abolitionist activist, delivered a groundbreaking speech in Viroqua. This talk marked the first women's rights address ever given in the Great Northwest. The event was pivotal in the fight for equality and social justice. Unfortunately, the platform collapsed during Stone's speech, but she bravely continued, declaring, "So will this nation fall unless slavery is abolished!" This dramatic incident further solidified her reputation as a fearless advocate.

Eat!

THE DRIFTLESS CAFÉ
118 W Court St.
608-637-7778

THE WOOLLY BEAR TAPHOUSE
117 E Terhune St.
608-638-3962

MAYBE LATELY'S FOOD & MORE
117 N Main St.
608-638-8395

NORWEGIAN HOLLOW HIDEAWAY
E4533 Norwegian Hollow Rd.
608-637-7776

to Do!

HISTORIC TEMPLE THEATRE OF VIROQUA
116 S Main St.
608-637-8190

DRIFTLESS FOLK SCHOOL
224 WI-56
608-284-8524

DRIFTLESS ANGLER
106 S Main St.
608-637-8779

Visit!

DRIFTLESS BOOKS AND MUSIC
518 Walnut St.
608-638-2665

VIROQUA PUBLIC MARKET
215 S Main St.
608-637-1912

GARY'S ROCK SHOP
317 S Main St.
608-637-7700

Stay!

HOTEL FORTNEY
100 N Main St.
608-638-3100

VIROQUA WAREHOUSE
504 E Decker St.
651-332-4431

VIROQUA HERITAGE INN
217 E Jefferson St.
608-637-3306

DRIFTLESS ANGLER FLY SHOP APARTMENT
106 S Main St.
608-637-8779

DRIFTLESS CREEK CABINS AND RETREAT CENTER
E7084 Tainter Rd.

HEAD NORTH OUT OF VIROQUA on US-14 W/US-61 N/Main Street. Follow US-14 North to Westby.

WESTBY

Westby was founded by Norwegian immigrants from Biri and Gausdal in the late 1840s. Drawn by the Driftless Region's topography, reminiscent of their homeland, they established a community steeped in Scandinavian traditions. The city's namesake, Ole T. Westby, a Norwegian-born storekeeper and Civil War veteran, played a pivotal role in the town's early development.

The Norwegian language was prevalent in homes and businesses, and traditional customs were deeply ingrained in the community. The town's strong Norwegian identity is celebrated annually through the Syttende Mai festival, a showcase of music, dance, and traditional crafts.

The Westby House Inn & Lodge

TIP

At the Snowflake Ski Jumping Tournament, listen for the term "Yard Sale" when a jumper falls and their equipment scatters all over the hill.

Westby's Norwegian history is reflected in the sport of ski jumping. The Snowflake Ski Club, founded in 1922, has fostered a love for the sport in the community. The club's annual tournament, featuring the seventh-largest ski jump in North America, attracts world-class athletes and passionate fans. Westby's cold winters and hilly terrain have created the perfect conditions for ski jumping, making the town a renowned destination for this thrilling winter sport.

The county also lays claim to a unique architectural heritage. Vernon County possesses an impressive collection of round barns, more than any other county in the nation. These round structures emerged in the late 19th and early 20th centuries as farmers sought more efficient ways to manage livestock. Many of the county's round barns were constructed by Algie Shivers, an African American carpenter whose craftsmanship has become legendary.

Eat!

OLD TOWNE INN SUPPER CLUB
100 E Old Town Rd. #8201
608-634-3991

BORGENS CAFÉ
109 S Main St.
608-634-4003

HILLSBORO BREWING COMPANY
206 E Madison St., Hillsboro
608-489-7486

THE STOCKYARD GRILL & SALOON
202 Central Ave., Coon Valley
608-452-2600

Stay!

WESTBY HOUSE INN & LODGE
200 W State St.

COULEE CABINS
W984 Co. Rd. P
608-452-3042

HISTORIC PER & ANNE PAULSON CABIN

NORSKEDALEN NATURE & HERITAGE CENTER
N455 O Ophus Rd., Coon Valley
608-452-3424

Visit!

PEACEFUL VALLEY HAVEN
E9230 Peaceful Valley Rd.
Cashton
608-654-7822

RIDGE HISTORY PARK
N1794 Korn Clements Rd.
Bangor
608-783-6745

NORSKEDALEN'S THRUNEGAARDEN
(open by appointment)
E4465 Hwy. 14/61, Coon Valley
608-452-3424

TUNNELVILLE CLIFFS STATE NATURAL AREA
Tunnelville Rd., La Farge
888-936-7463

to Do!

DREGNE'S SCANDINAVIAN GIFTS
100 S Main St.
608-634-4414

NORSKEDALEN NATURE & HERITAGE CENTER
N455 O Ophus Rd., Coon Valley
608-452-3424

WILDCAT MOUNTAIN STATE PARK
E13660 WI-33, Ontario
608-337-4775

THE BIG OLD RED SHED
113 E State St.

FROM WESTBY, take WI-27 N. At the traffic circle, continue straight to stay on WI-27 N. Take WI-27 N into Sparta.

SPARTA

Sparta is celebrated as the "Bicycling Capital of America" due to its creation of the Elroy-Sparta State Trail. The biking trail represents Sparta's visionary conservation and outdoor recreation efforts. Originally a bustling railroad corridor, the line fell into disuse in the mid-20th century. Recognizing its potential, Sparta pioneered the rails-to-trails movement, transforming the abandoned railway into a public trail in 1967. This 32-mile route features three notable railroad tunnels, offering an extraordinary experience for cyclists and hikers. The trail's success inspired countless similar projects nationwide, solidifying the community's status as a trailblazing example of repurposing underutilized infrastructure.

Sparta's innovative spirit is evident throughout the area, from railroads and astronauts to roadside attractions. Donald Kent "Deke" Slayton is a renowned figure in American space exploration. After serving as a pilot in World War II, he pursued an aviation career and was selected as one of NASA's original Mercury Seven astronauts in 1959, served as the space program's director of flight crew operations, and was a member of the Apollo-Soyuz mission in 1975.

FAST Fiberglass is known for creating iconic fiberglass statues that decorate countless roadside attractions across the US. From giant road-tripping landmarks like ice cream cones, ears of corn, and the monumental muskie at Hayward's Fresh Water Fishing Hall of Fame, their molds create a wide range of larger-than-life figures. If you've seen a towering Paul Bunyan statue or a larger-than-life dinosaur at a tourist stop, there's a good chance it originated as a FAST fiberglass mold.

Eat!

GINNY'S CUPBOARD
127 N Water St.
608-269-6669

RUDY'S DRIVE-IN RESTAURANT
514 S Water St.
608-269-2011

MATSUMOTO RAMEN HOUSE
106 N Water St.
608-487-9888

DORSET VALLEY SCHOOLHOUSE RESTAURANT
26147 WI-71, Wilton
608-343-5889

to Do!

DEKE SLAYTON MEMORIAL SPACE AND BIKE MUSEUM
200 W Main St.
608-269-0033

THE MONROE COUNTY LOCAL HISTORY ROOM AND MUSEUM
200 W Main St.
608-269-8680

SPEED'S BICYCLE SHOP
1126 John St.
608-269-2315

ELROY-SPARTA STATE TRAIL
111 Milwaukee St.
608-269-4123

BEER SHOP
200 W Wisconsin St.
608-487-9800

Stay!

CABOOSE CABINS
1102 S Water St.
608-269-0444

JUSTIN TRAILS RESORT
7452 Kathryn Ave.
608-855-0282

GOD'S COUNTRY GETAWAYS
12833 Co. Hwy. XX
Norwalk
608-387-6305

Visit!

BEN BIKIN' SCULPTURE
101 E Wisconsin St.

FAST FIBERGLASS MOLD GRAVEYARD
14177 Co. Hwy. Q

PAUL & MATILDA WEGNER GROTTO
7788 Daylight Rd.

TIP

The Deke Slayton Memorial Space and Bicycle Museum houses an extraordinary treasure: the only piece of moon rock on display in Wisconsin.

LAKE SUPERIOR
NNESOTA
DULUTH
SUPERIOR
WASHBURN
APOSTLE ISLANDS
ASHLAND
IRONWOOD
CHEQUAMEGON NATIONAL FOREST
DANBURY
HAYWARD
PARK FALLS
LAND O' LAKES
EAGLE RIVER
NICOLET NATIONAL FOREST
KINSFORD
SPOONER
PHILLIPS
RHINELANDER
CAMERON
LADYSMITH
CROIX LLS
MEDFORD
MERRILL
ANTIGO
EW RICHMOND
WISCONSIN
CHIPPEWA FALLS
MENOMONIE
EAU CLAIRE
OCONTO FALLS
SHAWANO
MARSHFIELD
CLINTONVILLE
MONDOVI
NEILLSVILLE
STEVENS POINT
WHITEHALL
WISCONSIN RAPIDS
WAUPACA
BLACK RIVER FALLS
PETENWELL DAM
MISSISSIPPI RIVER
WAUTOMA
TOMAH
CASTLE ROCK LAKE
MONTELLO
LAKE WINNEBAG
LA CROSSE
NEW LISBON
SHEBO
WESTBY
WISCONSIN DELLS
REEDSBURG
PORTAGE
BARABOO
BEAVER DAM
RICHLAND CENTER
SAUK CITY
MENOMONEE FALLS
IOWA
LAKE MENDOTA
BOSCOBEL
MADISON
MILWAUKE
DODGEVILLE
STOUGHTON
LANCASTER
JANESVILLE
MONROE
DUBUQUE
ILLINOIS
MIC

SOUTH CENTRAL:

HIGH WIRES AND NATURAL WONDERS

Along with experiencing Wisconsin Dells, a road trip is an excellent option to get out of town and see the area. Wisconsin Dells, known for its water parks and family-friendly attractions, is also a geological wonderland. One of the best ways to experience the geology of Wisconsin Dells is by taking a guided duck tour or boat tour. These amphibious vehicles and boats provide a floating perspective on the towering sandstone cliffs, deep canyons, and winding rivers that characterize the area.

For an entertaining experience, visit the Circus World Museum in Baraboo. This world-renowned museum showcases the history of the circus with exhibits featuring vintage circus wagons, costumes, and memorabilia.

In Portage, visitors can discover the Indian Agency House, a historic site that served as a meeting place for Native American tribes and government officials during the 19th century. The site offers a glimpse into the complex relationship between Native Americans and European settlers in the region.

A short drive from Wisconsin Dells, Montello is home to a significant historical site associated with the famed naturalist John Muir. Muir, known for his advocacy for preserving wilderness areas, spent time in the Montello region during his early years.

Horicon Marsh, located near Beaver Dam, is the largest freshwater marsh in the US. This wetland ecosystem is a vital habitat for numerous plant and animal species, including migratory birds.

By combining these diverse experiences, visitors can better appreciate Wisconsin Dells and the surrounding areas.

TO START THE TOUR, **DOWNTOWN BEAVER DAM** and drive counter clockwise ending in Portage.

BEAVER DAM

Beaver Dam owes much of its character and identity to the sprawling Horicon Marsh. This vast wetland ecosystem has shaped the region's history and ecology. Initially, the area was a hunting ground for Native American tribes. European settlers arrived in the mid-19th century, drawn by the fertile lands for farming. However, much of the land proved unsuitable for agriculture, leading to the creation of the marsh. Recognizing the marsh's ecological importance, conservation efforts began in the early 20th century. The establishment of the Horicon National Wildlife Refuge marked a turning point, transforming the area from a "wasteland" to a sanctuary for countless bird species, particularly during migration.

While the of Horicon Marsh has defined Beaver Dam's outdoor allure, the city has also cultivated a cultural scene. Nancy Zieman, a name synonymous with sewing, built a formidable empire centered in Beaver Dam. Her journey began in the 1970s when she started a small notions business, Nancy's Notions, from her kitchen table. In 1982, Zieman launched her television show, *Sewing with Nancy*. Her straightforward, patient instruction and warm, engaging personality made sewing accessible to millions. Beaver Dam became the center of Zieman's sewing world. Her retail store became a haven for sewing enthusiasts. Beyond the shop, the town became a destination for sewing workshops, retreats, and events. Today, her legacy lives on through the Nancy Zieman Sewing Studio, a space that inspires and educates sewing enthusiasts.

Eat!

MULLIN'S SHORT STOP
641 N Ludington St.
Columbus
920-623-2080

CHILI JOHN'S CAFÉ
223 Front St.
920-885-4414

WALKER'S DINER & BAKERY
813 Park Ave.
920-885-9041

DAM CHICKEN
300 S Spring St.
920-392-7787

Stay!

HA WHITNEY INN
229 N Ludington St. #3
Columbus

THE AUDUBON INN
45 N Main St., Mayville
920-644-2087

THE RECTORY BED & BREAKFAST
835 Madison St.
920-219-9434

TIP

Bobby Hatfield, one-half of the Righteous Brothers, was born in Beaver Dam on August 10, 1940. He later moved to California, where he met his musical partner, Bill Medley.

Visit!

JAEGER MILL AT DANVILLE DAM
W11312 Elba St.
Columbus

HORICON MARSH EDUCATION & VISITOR CENTER
N7725 WI-28, Horicon
920-387-7893

COLUMBUS DOWNTOWN HISTORIC DISTRICT
608-957-6080

WALLDOG MURALS OF BEAVER DAM #1

to Do!

SCHULTZ'S CHEESE HAUS
N6312 US-151
920-885-3734

CHIPPY'S POPCORN
507 Madison St.
920-885-2676

NANCY ZIEMAN SEWING STUDIO
120 Front St.
920-356-9546

SASSY COW CREAMERY
W4192 Bristol Rd.
Columbus
608-837-7766

FROM BEAVER DAM, take WI-33 W. Turn right on County Road A. Turn left on County Road AW. Turn right onto WI-73 N. Turn left onto WI-44 S. Turn right onto County Road B. Turn right onto WI-22 N into Montello.

MONTELLO

Montello is a town deeply rooted in both natural beauty and historical significance. Its story intertwines with the life of renowned naturalist and conservationist John Muir. Muir spent his formative years in the wilderness of Wisconsin. Arriving from Scotland at age 11, he settled with his family in Marquette County, near the present-day town of Montello. The region's pristine lakes, forests, and prairies ignited a lifelong passion for nature within the young Muir.

Once a quarry, now Daggett Memorial Park

Here, he developed a deep connection to the natural world, observing its intricacies and marveling at its beauty. These early experiences laid the foundation for his later work advocating for wilderness preservation. While Muir's most famous accomplishments occurred in California, where he championed the preservation of Yosemite and other national parks, his Wisconsin roots were essential in cultivating his love for the natural world.

The John Muir Park State Natural Area, located in John Muir County Park, offers a glimpse into the environment that shaped Muir. Inspired by the renowned naturalist's life and work, the center not only serves as a hub for environmental education and outdoor recreation but it is also a one-of-a-kind experience for nature enthusiasts and conservationists. The center has a variety of programs and exhibits that highlight the area's ecology and history. It also serves as the perfect starting point for the John Muir Nature and History Route, guiding visitors to follow in Muir's footsteps and experience the natural beauty that inspired him.

Eat!

GERMANIA LONGBRANCH SALOON
W1936 Eagle Rd.,
Neshkoro
920-293-8448

MONTELLO BREWING COMPANY
201 Main St.
608-422-4433

MECAN RIVER OUTFITTERS & LODGE
WI-23, Princeton
920-295-3439

Visit!

JOHN MUIR MEMORIAL COUNTY PARK
N1424 Co. Rd. F
608-297-3017

OBSERVATORY HILL STATE NATURAL AREA
Gillette Avenue

WISCONSIN'S BIGGEST TREE
120 Central Ave.

MUIR PARK STATE NATURAL AREA
N860 Co. Rd. F
888-936-7463

TIP

One of the most famous and largest trees in Wisconsin is the Cottonwood, located on Highway 23 in Montello. Considered to be 200 to 300 years old, it stood when French voyageurs passed through this region.

Stay!

WHITE LAKE BEACH RESORT
N4785 19th Ave.
608-297-2278

BUFFALO LAKE CAMPING RESORT
555 Lake Ave.
608-297-2915

KILBY LAKE CAMPGROUND
N4492 Fern Ave.
608-297-2344

'TWEEN THE LAKES MOTEL
510 Underwood Ave.
609-297-8715

ADELINE'S HOUSE OF COOL
6613 Marine Ct.
Markesan
312-531-7558

to Do!

MONTELLO THEATER
30 E Montello St.
608-322-2329

RENDEZVOUS PADDLE & SPORTS
200 Main St.
608-297-2444

FROM MONTELLO, take WI-22 S, then turn right onto County Highway F. Turn right on County Highway O. Turn left toward WI-23 W/I-39 ALT. Slight left onto WI-23 W into Wisconsin Dells.

WISCONSIN DELLS

The Wisconsin Dells, a natural wonder renowned for its stunning rock formations, has transformed from a serene retreat to a vibrant entertainment center. The harmonious blend of historic charm and modern attractions, and the area's natural beauty make the Dells a one-of-a-kind destination.

Once a tranquil destination for nature enthusiasts, the Dells now has many thrilling water parks, exhilarating rides, and interactive experiences. Yet the area's rich history is still palpable. Iconic attractions like the Original Duck Boat Tours and the Dells Boat Tours continue to delight visitors of all ages. At the same time, historic landmarks such as the Kilbourn Dam provides a glimpse into the region's past.

The Dells of today are a far cry from the simpler days of yore, and many fondly recall attractions that have since vanished. The echoes of laughter from Fort Dells, books that came to life at Storybook Gardens, and the magic of Tommy Bartlett's water ski shows still linger in the hearts of those who experienced it. You may even spot a bumper sticker stuck to the back window of a vintage car.

The juxtaposition of the old and new is particularly evident downtown.

One of the many fudge shops downtown

Once bustling with local commerce, historic buildings now house trendy shops, restaurants, and entertainment venues. This combination creates a vibrant atmosphere, appealing to history buffs and thrill-seekers. Future generations will continue to be captivated by the magic of the Wisconsin Dells and cherish the memories of those who came before.

Eat!

THE DEL-BAR
800 Wisconsin Dells Pkwy.
608-253-1861

PAUL BUNYAN'S COOK SHANTY
411 State Hwy. 13
608-254-8717

ISHNALA SUPPER CLUB
S2011 Ishnala Rd., Lake Delton
608-253-1771

MR. PANCAKE
1405 Wisconsin Dells Pkwy.
608-253-3663

TIP

Wisconsin Dells's first fudge shop, Original Wisconsin Dells Fudge, continues to make fudge with the same homemade recipe as when it opened in 1962. Ingredients include Wisconsin whipping cream and butter.

Stay!

DELL CREEK MOTEL
501 Wisconsin Dells Pkwy.
608-253-7301

FITZGERALD'S MOTEL
530 Broadway Ave.
608-253-1651

ISLAND POINT RESORT
1251 Canyon Rd.
608-254-6245

BLACK HAWK MOTEL
720 Race St.
608-254-7770

Visit!

DELLS OF THE WISCONSIN RIVER STATE NATURAL AREA
888-936-7463

PARSON'S INDIAN TRADING POST
370 Wisconsin Dells Pkwy.
608-254-8533

to Do!

UPPER DELLS BOAT TOURS
107 Broadway
609-254-8555

BIG SKY DRIVE-IN THEATRE
N9199 Winnebago Rd.
608-254-8025

H. H. BENNETT STUDIO
215 Broadway Ave.
608-253-3523

ORIGINAL WISCONSIN DUCKS
1890 Wisconsin Dells Pkwy.
608-254-8751

WISCONSIN DEER PARK
2183 Wisconsin Dells Pkwy.
608-253-2041

FROM WISCONSIN DELLS, head west on WI-13. Turn right onto County Road H. Turn left on Main Street in Reedsburg.

REEDSBURG

The years of World War II were a defining period for Reedsburg, showcasing the community's resilience and unity. The town rallied behind the war effort in numerous ways. Farmers increased food production to meet the nation's wartime demands, and dairy farmers worked tirelessly to supply essential dairy products. Many local industries shifted gears and turned their focus to producing war materials, contributing significantly to the overall effort.

One facet of Reedsburg's wartime experience was its role as a prisoner of war camp. German prisoners were housed in the camp and employed in various capacities, including agricultural work. This experience presented challenges and opportunities for the community.

TIP

To learn more about Reedsburg's involvement in World War II and the POW camp, read *The Forgotten Camp: The Reedsburg Prisoner of War Camp.*

Eat!

BRANDING IRON ROADHOUSE
132 S Main St.
Lime Ridge
608-986-2807

DELI BEAN
266 E Main St.
608-524-3373

HILLSBORO DRIVE-IN
515 Lake St., Hillsboro
608-489-3663

GREENWOOD'S CAFÉ
116 S Walnut St.
608-524-6203

HILLSBORO BREWING CO.
206 E Madison St.
Hillsboro
608-489-7486

Stay!

HAY CREEK CABINS
S2720 Co. Rd. V
608-524-0071

SEPTEMBER FARMS B & B
S1472 McKinney Rd.
La Valle
608-985-7375

VALLEY SPRINGS FARM BED & BREAKFAST
E4681 Co. Rd. S
608-495-1096

to Do!

CARR VALLEY CHEESE CO.
S3797 Co. Rd. G, La Valle
609-985-8200

SPIRIT VALLEY ALPACAS
S593 Walts Dr., Wonewoc
712-254-7500

PAINTED FOREST
Painted Forest Dr.
Wonewoc
800-444-4861

PIONEER LOG VILLAGE & MUSEUM
E7882 State Hwy. 23/33
608-495-3499

Visit!

LAKE REDSTONE WATERFALL
E4451 Douglas Rd.
La Valle

LAKE REDSTONE COUNTY PARK
E4522 Douglas Rd.
La Valle

Following the war, Reedsburg embarked on a period of growth and development, successfully transitioning to a peacetime economy. The town's agricultural roots remained strong, but Reedsburg also diversified its economic base, attracting new industries and businesses and creating a promising future.

Today, Reedsburg retains its small-town charm while embracing modern conveniences. The historic downtown area, with its well-preserved buildings, houses many shops and restaurants. The annual Butter Festival, a nod to Reedsburg's past as the "Butter Capital of the World," draws crowds with its delicious offerings and lively atmosphere.

Beyond its rich history, Reedsburg fosters a thriving arts and culture scene. The Wormfarm Institute annually hosts the Farm/Art DTour, a complimentary self-guided excursion through 50 miles of scenic farmland in rural Sauk County. The route includes site-responsive artworks, pasture performances, roadside pottery, local food markets, and more.

Historic County Farm School District No. 11

FROM REEDSBURG, head east on WI-33. Continue through two traffic circles. Take the first exit at the third traffic circle, stay on WI-33, and enter Baraboo.

BARABOO

Baraboo is synonymous with the circus. The small town holds a well-deserved place in the circus's annals. Its history is intricately woven with the rise and evolution of the Ringling Brothers and Barnum & Bailey Circus.

The five Ringling brothers—Albert, Alfred T., Otto, Charles, and John—began their circus journey in Baraboo in 1884. What started as a modest venture with a single wagon swiftly blossomed into a global phenomenon. The city, serving as the circus's winter quarters, housed animals, equipment, and performers during the off-season, contributing to its international reach. Baraboo became a bustling center of circus activity. Trainloads of performers, animals, and props arrived and departed, giving the town a energy and vitality. The Ringlings' success brought economic prosperity to the area.

Beyond the Ringling Brothers, other circus figures and companies called Baraboo home. The Gollmar Brothers Circus, another prominent circus family, operated out of the city for several years. This circus heritage has solidified Baraboo's reputation as "Circus City."

Today, the legacy lives on. Circus World Museum, located in the Ringling Brothers' former winter quarters, showcases the city's circus history. The museum houses an impressive collection of artifacts, wagons, and memorabilia, attracting visitors from around the globe. Baraboo's connection to the circus is a cornerstone of its identity, and the city continues to celebrate its circus heritage through various events and activities, including the yearly circus parade.

Eat!

BROADWAY DINER
304 Broadway St.
608-356-3287

GEM CITY SALOON & EATERY
124 Ash St.
608-355-9100

LITTLE VILLAGE CAFÉ
146 Fourth Ave.
608-356-2800

Stay!

RINGLING HOUSE BED & BREAKFAST
201 Eighth St.
608-299-9708

AL. RINGLING MANSION
623 Broadway St.
608-448-7455

WILLOWOOD INN
S5509 Co. Rd. DL
608-356-5474

Visit!

OCHSNER PARK ZOO
903 Park St.
608-355-2760

INTERNATIONAL CRANE FOUNDATION
E11376 Shady Lane Rd.
608-356-9462

DEVIL'S LAKE STATE PARK
S5975 Park Rd.
608-356-8301

AL. RINGLING THEATRE
136 Fourth Ave.
608-356-8864

to Do!

CIRCUS WORLD
550 Water St.
608-356-8341

ABLEMAN'S GORGE STATE NATURAL AREA
59 WI-136, Rock Springs
888-936-7463

ALDO LEOPOLD CENTER
E13701 Levee Rd.
608-355-0279

INTERNATIONAL CLOWN HALL OF FAME AND RESEARCH CENTER
102 Fourth Ave.
608-852-6767

WISCONSIN BIG CAT RESCUE
305 Pine St., Rock Springs
608-524-5466

TIP

Founded in 1981, the Baraboo Candy Company's signature product, the Original Cow Pie, became an instant hit. It combines the perfect blend of pecans, caramel, and rich chocolate.

FROM BARABOO, travel WI-113 S. Turn right onto WI-78. Turn left onto US-12 E. You have arrived in Sauk City.

SAUK CITY

The Badger Army Ammunition Plant (BAAP) was a significant part of Sauk County's history and a cornerstone of the community's past, particularly during World War II. Constructed in 1942, the plant covered over 7,000 acres and employed thousands of workers. Its primary function was the production of nitrocellulose-based propellants for ammunition.

The BAAP played a crucial role in supporting the war effort. However, its operations also came with environmental risks. The plant's manufacturing processes generated hazardous waste, which posed challenges for the

TIP

In 1975 the Sauk Prairie Jaycees recognized the Sauk Prairie Area as the Cow Chip Capital of Wisconsin and organized the first State Cow Chip Throw.

community and the environment. When the plant closed, extensive efforts were made to clean up the site and remediate the contaminated areas.

Currently, the site of the former BAAP is undergoing redevelopment. Portions of the land have been transferred to the Wisconsin Department of Natural Resources to create the Sauk Prairie State Recreation Area, which provides outdoor recreational opportunities for the community.

Sauk City is more than a charming town. Culver's, the beloved fast-food chain known for its ButterBurgers and frozen custard, traces its roots to Sauk City. Founded by the Culver family in 1984, the original restaurant captured the hearts of locals with its commitment to quality food and exceptional service. This successful concept quickly expanded beyond the town's borders, laying the foundation for the nationwide phenomenon it is today.

Eat!

GREEN ACRES
7487 WI-78
608-643-2305

ON THE ROX
8901 Co. Hwy. Y
608-370-7000

MERRIMAC FERRY LANDING CONCESSIONS
217 Wisconsin St.
Merrimac
608-393-2168

DORF HAUS SUPPER CLUB
8931 Co. Hwy. Y
608-643-3980

Visit!

MUSEUM OF BADGER ARMY AMMUNITION
7560 US-12, North Freedom
608-448-0244

GIBRALTAR ROCK STATE NATURAL AREA
Gibraltar Rock Rd., Lodi

SAUK CITY RIVERFRONT PARK
236 Water St.

SUSIE THE DUCK PARK
196 S Main St., Lodi
608-592-7474

Stay!

LUCKY'S BRIDGE MOTEL
W11585 Co. Rd. V, Lodi
608-592-5599

BURHOP'S LAKESIDE LODGE
W11610 Co. Rd. V, Lodi
608-592-4802

CEDARBERRY INN
855 Phillips Blvd.
608-643-6625

to Do!

MERRIMAC FERRY
236 Wisconsin St.
Merrimac

BUTTERCREAM BAKERY
112 S Main St., Lodi
608-592-0777

WOLLERSHEIM WINERY & DISTILLERY
7876 WI-188
Prairie du Sac
608-643-6515

BENDER'S BLUFFVIEW ANOE RENTALS
E10032 Huerth Rd.
608-544-2906

FROM SAUK CITY, take US-12 BUS/Water Street North. Continue straight onto WI-78. Turn left onto WI-113 N. Turn right onto County Road DL. Turn left onto WI-78 N. WI-78 turns slightly and becomes I-39 N. Take exit 87 for WI-33 E.

PORTAGE

Portage, a city along the scenic Wisconsin River, presents an unexpected fusion of experiences. Its strategic location makes it a convenient hub for winter sports enthusiasts. The Cascade Mountain ski area is famous throughout Wisconsin. With various trails suitable for all skill levels, this resort provides a fun-filled day on the slopes. Whether you're a seasoned skier or a beginner, Cascade Mountain has something for everyone.

Returning to Portage after a day on the slopes, visitors can indulge in another local delight: popcorn. Craig's Popcorn Corner is a beloved local institution. This corner shop makes a delightful array of popcorn flavors that have captured the taste buds of residents and visitors. Craig's Popcorn Corner has a flavor for every palate, from classic popcorn topped with butter, caramel, or cheddar cheese to more adventurous options like chocolate-covered popcorn. It's the perfect way to add a delicious treat to your day.

Beyond skiing and popcorn, you can find engaging local history in Portage. The Historic Indian Agency House, built in 1832, served as the residence of John and Juliette Kinzie, John was the US Indian agent to the Ho-Chunk Nation. This beautifully preserved building provides a glimpse into life on the frontier and the complex relationship between European settlers and Native Americans.

Whether seeking outdoor adventure, indulging your taste buds, or exploring the past, Portage offers a memorable experience.

Visit!

MACKENZIE CENTER
W7303 Co. Rd. C & Q
Poynette
608-635-8112

PAUQUETTE PARK
800 W Conant St.
608-742-7697

HISTORIC INDIAN AGENCY HOUSE
1490 Agency House Rd.
608-742-6362

FORT WINNEBAGO SURGEONS QUARTERS
1824 WI-33
608-742-2949

GIANT FARMER BOB
N5755 WI-78
608-356-8113

MAN MOUND PARK
E13087 Man Mound Rd.
Baraboo

Eat!

CIMAROLI'S SUPPER CLUB
W11793 WI-127
608-742-2238

LITTLE ITALY
2653 New Pinery Rd.
608-566-1232

SUZY'S STEAK & SEAFOOD HOUSE
2711 Co. Hwy. CX
608-742-8400

DINO'S RESTAURANT & LOUNGE
2900 New Pinery Rd.
608-742-4111

to Do!

CRAIG'S POPCORN CORNER
206 W Wisconsin St.
608-742-8050

MUSEUM AT THE PORTAGE
804 MacFarlane Rd.
608-742-6682

DURWARD'S GLEN RETREAT CENTER
W11876 McLeisch Rd., Baraboo
608-356-8113

PRAIRIE FLOWER BEADS
210 West Cook St.
608-742-5900

CASCADE MOUNTAIN
W10441 Cascade Mountain Rd.
608-742-5588

Giant Farmer Bob

TIP

Craig's Popcorn Corner also offers Chocolate Shoppe ice cream, a Wisconsin tradition since 1962, when Chuck Sr. and Nancy Deadman opened their candy and ice cream shop in Madison.

LAKE SUPERIOR
APOSTLE ISLANDS
WASHBURN
ASHLAND
IRONWOOD
CHEQUAMEGON NATIONAL FOREST
MICHIGAN
MARQUETTE
LAND O' LAKES
EAGLE RIVER
PARK FALLS
NICOLET NATIONAL FOREST
KINSFORD
PHILLIPS
RHINELANDER
LADYSMITH
GREEN BAY
MERRILL
MEDFORD
ANTIGO
NORTHERN DOOR COUNTY
MARINETTE
EGG HARBOR
WISCONSIN
OCONTO FALLS
DOOR PENINS
STURGEON BAY
SHAWANO
AU CLAIRE
MARSHFIELD
CLINTONVILLE
STEVENS POINT
NEILLSVILLE
GREEN BAY
DE PERE
HALL
BLACK RIVER FALLS
WISCONSIN RAPIDS
WAUPACA
PETENWELL DAM
WAUTOMA
MANITOWOC
TOMAH
CASTLE ROCK LAKE
LAKE WINNEBAGO
LA CROSSE
NEW LISBON
SHEBOYGAN
WESTBY
PORTAGE
BEAVER DAM
RICHLAND CENTER
LAKE MICHIGA
MENOMONEE FALLS
BOSCOBEL
LAKE MENDOTA
MADISON
MILWAUKEE
DODGEVILLE
STOUGHTON
LANCASTER
RACINE
JANESVILLE
MONROE
KENOSHA
DUBUQUE
ILLINOIS

GREEN BAY AND THE DOOR COUNTY COASTAL BYWAY

From remarkable shoreline views to plentiful fruit orchards, a road trip through the Green Bay region delivers a scenic journey through various landscapes. The name "Green Bay" is believed to be derived from the color of the water in the bay. Early French explorers described the water as having a greenish hue. Picturesque towns and villages surround this expansive body of water.

The region's history dates back to Native American tribes inhabiting the area. European explorers arrived in the 17th century, establishing trading posts and settlements. The region's strategic location on the Great Lakes made it a vital hub for the fur trade, timber, and shipping.

The Green Bay region has many varieties of historical attractions. Heritage Hill State Historical Park provides a glimpse into the past with restored buildings representing various eras. At the same time, Door County Maritime Museum showcases the region's connection to the Great Lakes shipping industry. Take Door County Coastal Byway to see the area's Scandinavian heritage, fishing industry, and artistic traditions.

In Shawano, discover the sturgeon, a prehistoric fish with an ancient lineage, which has long been a symbol of the area's waters. These creatures have played a significant role in the region's history and culture. Native Americans revered the sturgeon, and early European settlers recognized their commercial value, particularly for their caviar.

TO START THE TOUR, **MARINETTE** and drive around Green Bay ending in Door County.

MARINETTE

Located in Marinette County, "Wisconsin's Waterfall Capital," the small town of Marinette sits on the western shore of Green Bay and borders Michigan's Upper Peninsula. The area's original inhabitants were members of the Algonquin tribe, known as "the wild rice people." Additionally, the area's strategic location at the mouth of the Menominee River drew early French explorers and fur traders. The city's namesake originated from Marinette Chevalier, a French Chippewa Metis whose influence as a trader solidified the area's importance. However, the lumber boom of the late 19th century truly shaped Marinette's destiny. Sawmills sprang up along the river, transforming the town into a bustling industrial hub. The lumber barons who built fortunes during this era left an enduring mark on the city's architecture and infrastructure. The Lauerman brothers were also prominent figures in this era, contributing significantly to the city's economic growth.

As Marinette evolved, so did its culinary scene. Since 1942, Mickey-Lu-Bar-B-Q has been a local institution, serving up mouthwatering charcoal-broiled hamburgers that have garnered a cult following.

While the lumber industry has diminished, Marinette's history lives on. Stephenson Island Park, named after influential lumberman and US senator

Isaac Stephenson, gives a glimpse into the city's lumbering past. Marinette's past remains a cornerstone of its identity. The city's rich history is preserved in its museums and historical landmarks, allowing visitors to glimpse into the lives of those who came before.

> **TIP**
>
> Discover Marinette's history at the former Lauerman's Department Store. This century-old landmark, which opened in 1890 and closed in 1987, is now listed on the National Register of Historic Places.

Eat!

MICKEY-LU BAR-B-Q
1710 Marinette Ave.
715-735-7721

IRONWORKS ON MAIN
1333 Main St.
715-504-2000

THE RIVER'S EDGE SUPPER CLUB
N4178 WI-180 Trunk
715-735-7344

BLUE BIKE BURRITO
2020 Hall Ave.
715-735-9889

Visit!

STEPHENSON ISLAND PARK
1680 Bridge St.
715-732-5140

DAVE'S FALLS COUNTY PARK
Old 141 Rd., Amberg

MCCLINTOCK COUNTY PARK
N14251 Co. Rd. I
Athelstane

LONG SLIDE FALLS COUNTY PARK
Lone Slide Rd., Niagara

Stay!

LAUERMAN HOUSE INN
1975 Riverside Ave.
715-732-7800

M & M VICTORIAN INN
1393 Main St.
715-732-7800

GOVERNOR SCOFIELD BED & BREAKFAST
610 Main St., Oconto
920-834-3846

GOODMAN PARK CAMPGROUND CABIN
N15201 Goodman Park Rd., Athelstane
marinettecountywi.gov

to Do!

BAYER HOME AND CARRIAGE MUSEUM
917 Park Ave., Oconto
920-834-6206

MOUNTAIN FIRE LOOKOUT TOWER
Mountain Tower Rd.
Mountain

LUMBERJACK STEAM TRAIN & CAMP 5 MUSEUM
5068 US-8, Laona
715-674-3414

PESHTIGO FIRE MUSEUM
400 Oconto Ave., Peshtigo
715-582-3244

Eat where the locals eat.

TRAVEL WEST FROM MARINETTE on WI-64. Turn left on WI-55 S. Continue on WI-55 S into downtown Shawano.

SHAWANO

The Menominee people, original inhabitants of the Shawano area, had a deep-rooted connection to the Wolf River and its sturgeon. These fish were a vital part of their diet and culture. Sturgeon provided sustenance, tools, and materials for clothing. Their spiritual significance was also profound, often incorporated into ceremonies and stories. This rich history continues to influence the region's appreciation for the sturgeon and the importance of preserving their habitat.

Shawano is famous for its annual Lake Sturgeon spawning spectacle. Thousands of these ancient fish gather in the Wolf River to reproduce every spring. This natural wonder draws visitors from far and wide to witness the incredible sight of hundreds of sturgeon congregating in a single area. Sturgeon Park offers a prime viewing spot for this extraordinary event.

Nearby, River Haven on the Wolf is a historic lodge built in 1873 along the banks of the scenic Wolf River. Originally serving as a logger's retreat, it has been lovingly restored while preserving its rustic charm. Nature enthusiasts, anglers, and those seeking a taste of the region's history will find a serene escape here.

TIP

In Shawano, visit the iconic Sun Drop University to witness the bottling process, enjoy free samples, explore interactive displays, and shop at the Sun Drop gift shop.

The Sun Drop Museum and Gift Shop

While exploring the history of Shawano, a short drive to Clintonville is worthwhile. The FWD Seagrave Museum showcases the history of the Four Wheel Drive Auto Company, a pioneer in all-wheel-drive technology. Home to over 80 historic trucks, including the first successful four-wheel drive vehicle, the museum delivers a fascinating glimpse into automotive innovation.

Post office art commissioned under President Franklin D. Roosevelt's New Deal

Eat!

FARM INN ON MAIN
123 N Main St.
715-524-4916

HURRICANE DAWN'S
W11057 Co. Rd. D, Marion
715-754-5138

STUBBORN BROTHERS BREWERY
220 S Main St.
715-201-0859

CRUISE IN
549 E Prospect Ave., Marion
715-973-1034

Stay!

RIVER HAVEN ON THE WOLF
N2610 Log Cabin Dr., White Lake
920-254-4358

PINEWOOD COTTAGES
W5409 N Shore Dr.
262-321-8737

to Do!

SUN DROP UNIVERSITY IN TWIG'S MUSEUM AND GIFT SHOP
920 S Franklin St.
715-526-5031

FWD SEAGRAVE MUSEUM
325 15th St., Clintonville
715-823-4011

SHAWANO SKI SHARKS WATERSKI SHOW
211 Riverside Dr.

Visit!

MENOMINEE LOGGING CAMP MUSEUM
W3426 Co. Rd. VV W, Keshena
715-799-3757

OLD GLORY CANDY
126 S Main St.
715-526-3253

BELLE PLAINE CHEESE FACTORY
N3473 Wisconsin Ave.
715-526-2789

HERITAGE PARK
524 N Franklin St.
715-526-3323

STURGEON PARK
801 S Water St.
715-526-6171

"THE FIRST SETTLERS" HISTORICAL MURAL
Shawano Post Office Lobby
235 S Main St.

GO EAST on WI-55/WI-22. Continue on WI-22 E. Turn right on WI-29 BUS. In Bonduel, turn right on WI-29/WI-47. Turn left on WI-156. Turn right on North Countryline Road. Turn left on Trout Creek Road. Turn left on Riverdale Drive. Right on County Road RK. Left on Shawano Avenue into Green Bay.

GREEN BAY

Green Bay has plenty of exceptional experiences with the region's outdoor activities and history. As one of the oldest settlements in the Midwest, its story begins with the arrival of French explorers in the 17th century.

Named after the emerald bay at its heart, Green Bay was a crucial trading post for French fur traders. The confluence of the Fox and Wisconsin rivers provided a vital water route to the Great Lakes, making Green Bay a strategic location. After the American Revolution, Americans built Fort Howard to protect the entryway into Wisconsin. Over time, the area became a melting pot of cultures, with Native American, French, and English influences shaping its development.

Historic Hotel Northland in Downtown Green Bay

The decline of the lumber industry in the early 20th century forced the city to diversify its economy. Meanwhile, the world breathed a sigh of relief in 1935 with the introduction of splinter-free toilet paper from "the toilet paper capital of the world." Green Bay also boasts Wisconsin's first newspaper, the *Green Bay Intelligencer*, which began in 1833. It was also the first Wisconsin city to receive mail.

Green Bay has a diverse range of historical attractions. Heritage Hill State Historical Park transports visitors back in time with its historic homes and shops. The Hotel Northland, a restored Art Deco masterpiece, showcases the city's elegant past. For family fun, Bay Beach Amusement Park provides classic rides and nostalgic charm, making it a favorite local spot.

TIP

Step back in time and experience affordable fun at Bay Beach Amusement Park in Green Bay. Enjoy free parking, admission, and classic rides like the Zippin Pippin rollercoaster, once a favorite of Elvis.

Eat!

AL'S HAMBURGER
131 S Washington St.
920-437-5114

KROLL'S EAST
1658 Main St.
920-468-4422

CAPTAIN'S WALK WINERY
345 S Adams St.
920-431-9255

Visit!

AMELIA CORNELIUS CULTURE PARK
1250 Packerland Dr.
920-496-5384

THE AUTOMOBILE GALLERY & EVENT CENTER
400 S Adams St.
920-437-9024

BAY BEACH WILDLIFE SANCTUARY
1660 E Shore Dr.
920-391-3671

PACKERS HERITAGE TRAIL
1265 Lombardi Ave.
920-569-7512

GREEN BAY PACKERS HALL OF FAME & MUSEUM
1265 Lombardi Ave.
920-569-7512

to Do!

BAY BEACH AMUSEMENT PARK
1313 Bay Beach Rd.
920-448-3365

HERITAGE HILL STATE HISTORICAL PARK
2640 S Webster Ave.
920-448-5150

MEYER THEATRE
117 S Washington St.
920-433-3333

NEVILLE PUBLIC MUSEUM
210 Museum Pl.
920-448-4460

TURNER STREET MUSIC HALL
437 Turner St.
Wrightstown
920-857-4475

Stay!

HOTEL NORTHLAND
304 N Adams St.
920-393-7499

ASTOR HOUSE BED AND BREAKFAST
637 S Monroe Ave.
920-432-3585

LEAVING DOWNTOWN GREEN BAY, head southeast on East Walnut Street. Turn right onto South Monroe Avenue/ Wisconsin Firefighters and EMT Highway. Continue into DePere.

TIP

Immerse yourself in Oneida history and culture at the Oneida Nation Museum. Explore captivating exhibits, learn about rich traditions, and discover the heart of Oneida agriculture at the Three Sisters Garden.

National Railroad Museum

DE PERE

De Pere's story begins in 1671, when Jesuit missionary Father Claude-Jean Allouez established the mission of Rapides des Pères ("Rapids of the Fathers"), which later evolved into De Pere. The city's strategic location on the Fox River made it a vital trading post for French fur traders. The convergence of Native American, French, and English cultures shaped the region's early development. As the 19th century dawned, De Pere experienced rapid growth fueled by the lumber industry.

The Union Hotel, a De Pere staple since 1883, holds an intriguing history. Initially a two-story building with "fire-proof" features, it has evolved into a popular supper club. Its location in the heart of De Pere adds charm, making it a cherished part of the community's heritage. The hotel holds a piece of Packers history, as the team logo was partially designed on-site by long-time resident and equipment manager Gerald "Dad" Braisher. However, making room reservations requires old-fashioned patience. Reservations can be made only by phone or in person at the desk. If no one answers, just leave a message, and someone will return your call. The hotel does not use voicemail or its website to make bookings.

De Pere's historical sites are unparalleled. The National Railroad Museum showcases historic trains, while District 82 Pinball Museum provides nostalgic fun. For a cultural experience, visit the Oneida Nation Museum to learn about the heritage of the local Native American tribe.

Eat!

THE UNION HOTEL & RESTAURANT
200 N Broadway
920-336-6131

COLONIAL HOUSE SUPPER CLUB
N4330 Co. Rd. E
Kaukauna
920-788-2622

THE EXCHANGE COFFEE, MERCANTILE & EATERY
317 Main Ave.
Luna Coffee Roasters
330 Main Ave.

HOTEL SEYMOUR SUPPERCLUB
210 S Main St., Seymour
920-833-6441

Visit!

ONEIDA NATION MUSEUM
W892 Co. Rd. EE
920-869-2768

ONEIDA NATION APPLE ORCHARD
3976 W Mason St., Hobart
920-869-2468

SCRAY CHEESE
2082 Old Martin Rd.
920-347-0303

HAMBURGER HALL OF FAME
133 Depot St., Seymour
920-833-6688

BROWN COUNTY FONFEREK'S GLEN
2825 Dutchman Rd.
Green Bay
920-448-6242

POLO-RESTO
201 William St.

to Do!

DISTRICT 82 PINBALL ARCADE
800 O'Keefe Rd., Suite F
920-621-9631

NATIONAL RAILROAD MUSEUM
2285 S Broadway
Ashwaubenon
920-437-7623

FIELD OF SCENES
N3712 WI-55, Freedom

Stay!

THE UNION HOTEL & RESTAURANT
200 N Broadway
920-336-6131

FROM DE PERE, travel on WI-57. Continue on WI-57/WI-42 N. Turn left on South Lansing Avenue. Turn right on Green Bay Road. Follow South Madison Avenue to downtown Sturgeon Bay.

The Union Hotel and Restaurant in De Pere

STURGEON BAY

Sturgeon Bay benefits from its strategic location on the Door County Peninsula. Fishing became a primary industry, supporting local families and contributing to the region's economy. However, as the 19th century progressed, the focus shifted toward maritime commerce. Sturgeon Bay's deep harbor and location on the Great Lakes made it an ideal location for shipyards. The city flourished as a shipbuilding center, and the Great Lakes shipping industry relied heavily on Sturgeon Bay for ship repairs and construction. While shipbuilding has declined, Sturgeon Bay continues to embrace its nautical roots through tourism, fishing, and water-related activities.

Reflecting this maritime heritage, the Door County Maritime Museum delves into the region's nautical history. For stunning scenery, visit Sherwood Point Lighthouse or hike through Cave Point County Park, which is known for its spectacular geological formations. And don't miss the chance to tour the tug John Purves, a floating exhibit docked at the Maritime Museum.

TIP

Experience the thrill of seeing colossal ships up close as they arrive for winter repairs in Sturgeon Bay. This seasonal opportunity allows you to witness these maritime marvels like never before.

The retro Holiday Music Motel is a Sturgeon Bay icon for a unique place to stay. Initially a classic motel built in 1952, it transformed into a music haven in 2009 due to musical artists banding together each year while working to save the Sturgeon Bay Bridge. The hotel hosts songwriting retreats, live music, and even a radio station broadcasting original music created in the motel.

Eat!

DONNY'S GLIDDEN LODGE RESTAURANT
4670 Glidden Dr.
920-746-9460

MORNING GLORY BY THE BAY
306 S Third Ave.
920-818-0711

BLUEFRONT CAFÉ
86 W Maple St.
920-743-9218

Stay!

HOLIDAY MUSIC HOTEL
30 N First Ave.
920-743-5571

CHANTICLEER CABINS
4017 Cherry Rd.
920-493-2395

THE SCOFIELD HOUSE
908 Michigan St.
920-743-7727

Visit!

CAVE POINT COUNTY PARK
5360 Schauer Rd.
920-746-9959

STURGEON BAY CANAL PIERHEAD LIGHTHOUSE AND CANAL LIGHT
2501 Canal Rd.

CHOICE ORCHARDS
4594 Co. Rd. HH
92 0-743-8980

THE GARDEN DOOR
4312 WI-42
920-746-2260

RENARD'S CHEESE
2189 Co. Rd. DK
920-825-7272

POPELKA TRENCHARD GALLERY & GLASS STUDIO
64 S Second Ave.
920-743-7287

to Do!

THIRD AVENUE PLAYWORKS
239 N Third Ave.
920-743-1760

DOOR COUNTY MARITIME MUSEUM
120 N Madison Ave.
920-743-5958

RAY AND RUTHIE STONECIPHER ASTRONOMY CENTER
2200 Utah St.
920-746-5895

FROM STURGEON BAY, Take WI-42 N. Turn right onto WI-57 N. Turn right onto WI-42/North Bay Shore Drive. Follow North Bay Shore Drive into Gills Rock.

Tempt your taste buds with a fish boil or cherry-stuffed french toast at the White Gull Inn.

NORTHERN DOOR COUNTY

Door County transformed dramatically in the 20th century. While the early years focused on lumber and agriculture, especially cherries, the latter half celebrated tourism. The county invested in preserving its natural beauty and developing recreational amenities, solidifying its reputation as a haven for outdoor lovers and artists.

As the lumber industry declined, cherry orchards emerged as a significant economic force. The county gained the moniker "Cherryland USA," as it supplied most of the nation's tart cherry crop. The distinctive soil and climate created ideal growing conditions for cherries, particularly the Montmorency variety. The cherry industry remains vital to the region's economy, with orchards offering pick-your-own experiences and a variety of cherry-inspired products.

Door County is also famous for its fish boils, a culinary tradition dating back to the region's Scandinavian settlers. This communal dining experience features freshly caught whitefish, potatoes, and onions cooked in a large outdoor cauldron. As the fish is added, a dramatic splash of kerosene ignites, creating a fiery spectacle. The meal is typically followed by cherry pie, a sweet ending to a memorable feast.

Several Door County restaurants are renowned for their fish boils. Pelletier's in Fish Creek, a longtime local favorite, provides a classic fish boil experience. The White Gull Inn, also in Fish Creek, has a more upscale setting for this traditional meal. For a charming atmosphere, consider the Old Post Office Restaurant in Ephraim, where you can enjoy a fish boil with a stunning view.

Eat!

WHITE GULL INN
4225 Main St., Fish Creek
920-868-3517

THE OLD POST OFFICE RESTAURANT
10040 N Water St., Ephraim
920-854-4034

WILSON'S RESTAURANT & ICE CREAM PARLOR
9990 Water St. S, Ephraim
920-854-2041

AL JOHNSON'S SWEDISH RESTAURANT & BUTIK
10698 N Bay Shore Dr.
Sister Bay
920-854-2626

Visit!

CAVE POINT COUNTY PARK
5360 Schauer Rd.
Sturgeon Bay
920-746-9959

ANDERSON DOCK
3083 Anderson Ln.
Ephraim
920-854-5501

DOOR COUNTY CURVY HIGHWAY
416-498 WI-42
Ellison Bay

WASHINGTON ISLAND STAVKIRKE
Town Line Rd.
Washington
920-847-2179

TIP

Northern Sky Theater is a must-see for anyone visiting Door County, including furry friends. Well-behaved dogs on leashes are welcome to attend the Summer State Park Amphitheater Shows.

Stay!

BLACKSMITH INN ON THE SHORE
8152 WI-57
Baileys Harbor
920-839-9222

THE WATER STREET INN
9944 Water St. S, Ephraim
920-854-2831

THE LIBERTY LODGE AT SISTER BAY
11034 WI-42
Sister Bay
920-854-2025

to Do!

OFF THE WHEEL POTTERY
4234 Co. Rd. E
Egg Harbor
920-868-9608

EAGLE BLUFF LIGHTHOUSE
10249 Shore Rd.
Fish Creek
920-421-2332

CANA ISLAND LIGHTHOUSE
8800 E Cana Island Rd.
Baileys Harbor
920-743-5958

PENINSULA PLAYERS THEATRE
4351 Peninsula Players Rd.
Fish Creek
920-868-3287

LAKE SUPERIOR
APOSTLE ISLANDS
MICHIGAN
MARQUETTE
WASHBURN
ASHLAND
IRONWOOD
CHEQUAMEGON NATIONAL FOREST
HAYWARD
PARK FALLS
LAND O' LAKES
EAGLE RIVER
NICOLET NATIONAL FOREST
KINSFORD
PHILLIPS
RHINELANDER
LADYSMITH
MERRILL
MEDFORD
ANTIGO
MARINETTE
WISCONSIN
CHIPPEWA FALLS
EAU CLAIRE
OCONTO FALLS
SHAWANO
STURGEON BAY
EGG HARBOR
MARSHFIELD
CLINTONVILLE
MONDOVI
NEILLSVILLE
STEVENS POINT
GREEN BAY
WHITEHALL
BLACK RIVER FALLS
WISCONSIN RAPIDS
WAUPACA
PETENWELL DAM
WAUTOMA
MANITOWOC
TOMAH
CASTLE ROCK LAKE
LAKE WINNEBAGO
LA CROSSE
NEW LISBON
SHEBOYGAN
WESTBY
PORTAGE
BEAVER DAM
RICHLAND CENTER
MENOMONEE FALLS
WATERTOWN
OCONOMOWOC
LAKE MENDOTA
BOSCOBEL
MADISON
WAUKESHA
DOWNTOWN MILWAUKEE
FORT ATKINSON
DODGEVILLE
LANCASTER
WHITEWATER
JANESVILLE
BURLINGTON
MONROE
DELAVAN
LAKE GENEVA
DUBUQUE
ILLINOIS

SOUTHEAST:

IMMIGRANTS, INNOVATION, AND SHOWMANSHIP

A great place to start is downtown Milwaukee, where you can see how 19th-century German immigrants shaped the city's culture. Begin your journey at Usinger's sausage shop, then see the Best Place at the Historic Pabst Brewery, the iconic Pabst Mansion, and the Pabst Theater.

Pabst Brewing Company significantly influenced the city's development and cultural landscape. Built between 1890 and 1892 for Captain Frederick Pabst, the Pabst Mansion, a majestic Italianate mansion, is now a museum open to the public. The Pabst Theater, another iconic landmark, has been a center of entertainment since its opening in 1889. Continue going west on Wisconsin Avenue for a remarkable historical experience.

While Milwaukee and Waukesha are neighboring cities, they each have unique cultural treasures. Waukesha is the home of Les Paul, a legendary guitarist and inventor whose innovations revolutionized the music industry.

Lake Geneva has been a popular destination for Chicagoans since the late 19th century. See the shoreline and learn about the area's history on the Lake Geneva Cruise Line. Delavan, another lake town, has a terrific circus history. During the winter months, when circus performances were less frequent, touring circus companies often set up their winter quarters in Delavan. Make sure to visit the downtown exhibits in Tower Park.

Oconomowoc takes pride in its involvement in the classic 1939 movie *The Wizard of Oz.* Walk the yellow brick road with the movie's life-size characters and read details about the city's role in the film for an immersive experience.

TO START THE TOUR, **DOWNTOWN MILWAUKEE** then drive west on W. Wisconsin Ave. to Waukesha and end in loop in Oconomowoc.

MILWAUKEE

Milwaukee has a history centered around brewing, entertainment, and culinary traditions. Milwaukee's reputation as a brewing capital began in the mid-19th century when German immigrants, skilled in the art of beer-making, settled in the area. The city's pure water from Lake Michigan proved ideal for brewing, and soon numerous breweries sprang up.

One of the most prominent names in Milwaukee's brewing history is Pabst. Founded in 1844 as Best & Company, the brewery was later renamed the Pabst Brewing Company under the leadership of Captain Frederick Pabst. The company rose to prominence in the late 19th century, becoming one of the largest breweries in the United States. Pabst Blue Ribbon, its flagship beer, became a national icon.

The Pabst family's influence extended beyond the brewing industry. Captain Pabst constructed the extravagant Pabst Mansion as a symbol of his success. Now, the mansion is a museum open to the public, offering a glimpse into the lavish lifestyle of the Gilded Age.

Another attribute to the Pabst family's cultural contributions is the Pabst Theater. Built in 1895, this magnificent theater is one of the oldest continuously operating theaters in the US. Its ornate interior and illustrious history make it a top Milwaukee landmark.

Waterfront dining at Barnacle Buds

Milwaukee's culinary scene is equally impressive, with Usinger's Sausage a standout example. Arriving in Milwaukee with $400 and a wealth of sausage-making knowledge, Frederick Usinger, a young German immigrant, started working at a local butcher shop. Usinger purchased the business, and in 1880, Usinger's Sausage was officially born.

to Do!

MILWAUKEE PUBLIC MUSEUM
800 W Wells St.
414-278-2728

STREETS OF OLD MILWAUKEE
800 W Wells St.
414-278-2702

PABST MANSION
2000 W Wisconsin Ave.
414-931-0808

THE PABST THEATER
144 E Wells St.
414-242-8200

BEST PLACE AT THE HISTORIC PABST BREWERY
917 W Juneau Ave.
414-630-1609

USINGER'S FAMOUS SAUSAGE
1030 N Doctor M.L.K. Jr. Dr.
414-276-9100

HISTORIC MILLER CAVES
3897 W State St.
414-931-2337

Eat!

MADER'S RESTAURANT
1041 N Doctor M.L.K. Jr. Dr.
414-271-3377

SAFEHOUSE
779 N Front St.
414-271-2007

MILWAUKEE BRAT HOUSE
1013 N Doctor M.L.K. Jr. Dr.
414-273-8709

FIVE O'CLOCK STEAKHOUSE
2416 W State St.
414-342-3553

JIZZLES SANDWICH SHOP
2611 W State St.
414-447-9780

Visit!

ST. JOAN OF ARC CHAPEL
1421 W Wisconsin Ave.
800-222-6544

Stay!

AMBASSADOR HOTEL MILWAUKEE
2308 W Wisconsin Ave.
414-345-5000

MANDERLEY BED & BREAKFAST INN
3026 W Wells St.
414-459-1886

TIP

Take a Miller Brewery tour to experience brewing history. See Frederick Miller's humble beginnings and explore the historic underground caves and the charming Bavarian-style Miller Inn.

FROM DOWNTOWN MILWAUKEE, take Wisconsin Avenue west. Turn left on I-94 ALT/WI-100. Exit right on West Blue Mound Road. Turn left on North Sunny Slope Road. Turn right on WI-59/West Greenfield Avenue. Continue on Arcadian Avenue and turn right on Pleasant Street, arriving on Waukesha's Main Street.

WAUKESHA

Waukesha has a storied past consisting of natural resources, Cold War tensions, and musical innovation. Furthermore, Waukesha is renowned for its natural springs. The late 19th and early 20th centuries marked a golden age for Waukesha, often called the "Saratoga of the West." The discovery of the healing properties of Waukesha's mineral-rich waters in the 1860s sparked a frenzy of activity. Belief in the curative powers of these waters, prevalent during the Victorian era, drew thousands of visitors seeking relief from various ailments. Elaborate bottling plants, ornate springhouses, and luxurious resorts sprung up to accommodate the influx of visitors. Waukesha became a bustling hub of social activity, attracting the wealthy and famous.

The dynamic social scene that characterized Waukesha's early decades yielded to a more somber atmosphere as the city assumed a crucial role in national defense during the Cold War. The city was home to a Nike missile site, part of a network designed to protect against potential aerial threats. While the site is no longer active, remnants of this era can still be found in Hillcrest Park.

TIP

Les Paul found his final resting place in Prairie Home Cemetery. Visit his grave marker and the 500-square-foot granite monument with his inscribed biography and awards.

Les Paul mural across the street from the old train depot

Waukesha's history spans from Cold War technology to musical genius. Growing up in Waukesha, Les Paul experimented with sound, building his own instruments and tinkering with electronics. Paul's inventive nature and love for technology were instrumental in developing the solid-body electric guitar, reshaping the sound of popular music. His early fascination would eventually lead to revolutionary advancements in the world of recording and guitar design.

La Estacion Mexican Restaurant is located in the former train depot.

Stay!

THE INN
N4W22496 Bluemound Rd.
414-915-7565

THE CLARKE HOTEL
314 W Main St.
262-549-3800

Eat!

LA ESTACION
319 Williams St.
262-521-1986

JIMMY'S GROTTO
314 E Main St.
262-542-1500

JOHN'S DRIVE-IN
1317 Arcadian Ave.
262-542-2842

THE STEAMING CUP
340 W Main St.
262-522-3605

ROCHESTER DELI
143 W Broadway
262-522-9611

Visit!

NIKE MISSLE CONTROL SITE M-74 IN HILLCREST PARK
2119 Davidson Rd.
262-548-8898

HOBO SPRING
1376 Frame Park Dr.

FRAME PARK FORMAL GARDENS
1150 Frame Park Dr.
262-524-3737

LES PAUL MONUMENT
605 S Prairie Ave.
262-524-3540

LES PAUL PERFORMANCE CENTER
321 Wisconsin Ave.
262-522-9356

to Do!

TEN CHIMNEYS
S43 W31575 Depot Rd.
262-968-4161

WAUKESHA COUNTY HISTORICAL SOCIETY & MUSEUM
101 W Main St.
262-521-2859

WAUKESHA CIVIC THEATRE
264 W Main St.
262-547-0708

FROM WAUKESHA, follow S East Ave south. Continue on WI-164 south. Turn right onto WI-36 S. Veer left onto US-83. Exit at US-36 BUS and continue into Burlington.

BURLINGTON

Burlington's McCanna & Fraser Co. was known mainly for its role in the production of condensed milk. The company was founded by Charles B. McCanna in 1882, quickly becoming a major force in Wisconsin's dairy industry. To support its operations, McCanna bought 15 refrigerated railcars, established a tin can factory in 1902, and established a cold storage plant in the same year.

The company's products were distributed nationwide under the "Lion Brand" label, with a significant portion of its output destined for international markets. Condensed milk, a concentrated form of milk with an extended shelf life, was a popular product in the late 19th and early 20th centuries. It was widely used in households for baking, for cooking, and as a beverage.

Condensed milk produced in Burlington became a pantry staple nationwide, but the city's reputation would be further sweetened by a

TIP

B. J. Wentker's, one of Burlington's most photographed places, was started by German immigrant Bernard J. Wentker in 1894. Allegedly, the tavern operated as an ice cream parlor during Prohibition.

Grab a coffee at one of Burlington's historic downtown buildings.

different dairy product. Burlington proudly earned the title of "Chocolate City, USA," thanks to the establishment of a Nestlé chocolate factory in 1966. The city embraced its new nickname with enthusiasm, hosting annual chocolate festivals and events and even having a chocolate museum. Burlington's Chocolate Museum, which closed in 2023, once offered a delightful exploration of chocolate history featuring exhibits such as chocolate sculptures and interactive displays.

While the Nestlé factory has undergone changes, including a shift from chocolate to cookie dough, the city's chocolate heritage remains a cherished part of its identity. Although Burlington is exploring a new brand image, the legacy of the "Chocolate City" remains.

FROM BURLINGTON, turn left on McHenry Street. Continue straight to stay on McHenry Street. Turn right onto WI-50 W and follow into Lake Geneva.

Stay!

LILY LAKE RESORT
7910 328th Ave.
262-537-2848

ALPINE VALLEY RESORT
W2501 Co. Rd. D
Elkhorn
262-642-7374

Visit!

W. R. WADEWITZ NATURE CAMP
2716 Buena Park Rd.

Eat!

B. J. WENTKER'S
230 Milwaukee Ave.
262-758-6112

BOMB BURGER
532 McHenry St.

THE MAIN EVENT
556 N Pine St.
262-763-8863

BLACKBIRD BAKERY
256 E Chestnut St., Suite A
262-661-4029

FRED'S PARKVIEW
596 N Pine St.
262-763-8370

NAPOLI RESTAURANT AND PIZZERIA
132 N Pine St.
262-763-8390

THE COFFEE HOUSE AT CHESTNUT & PINE
492 N Pine St.
262-661-4394

NOBLE BROTHERS WATERFORD CREAMERY AND BURGER SHOP
100 S Jefferson St.
Waterford
262-534-4757

to Do!

MALT HOUSE THEATRE
109 N Main St.
262-763-9873

PEDAL & CUP
1722 WI-120, Lake Geneva
262-249-1111

RICHARD BONG STATE RECREATION AREA
26313 Burlington Rd.
Kansasville
262-878-5600

READS BY THE RIVER BOOKS AND GIFTS
102 E Main St., Waterford
262-720-7323

LAKE GENEVA

The late 19th century marked a transformative period for Lake Geneva. Wealthy Chicagoans seeking escape from the bustling city discovered the area's natural beauty and built luxurious summer homes. This influx of affluent residents earned Lake Geneva the nickname "Newport of the West." The Great Chicago Fire of 1871 accelerated the area's growth, as many displaced residents sought refuge in their lakefront retreats. The town's infrastructure expanded to accommodate the increasing number of visitors, and Lake Geneva solidified its reputation as a premier resort destination.

Go back in time at Grandma Vickie's Cafe.

One of the cornerstones of this resort experience is the Lake Geneva Cruise Line, a historic passenger boat line offering a unique and unforgettable way to explore the lake's beauty. With a fleet of eight boats, each with its own unique appeal, the cruise line offers a variety of options. The Lake Geneva Mailboat is a one-of-a-kind adventure that combines scenic cruising with a touch of nostalgia. This tradition has been a hallmark of Lake Geneva summers for over a century. As the boat navigates the lake, passengers are treated to stunning views of lavish estates, historic landmarks, and the area's elegance. The mail carrier's daring jumps from the moving boat to deliver mail are a thrilling spectacle that has made the Lake Geneva Mailboat a popular tourist attraction. While delivering mail, the cruise also provides a peaceful and enlightening excursion, complete with onboard narration about Lake Geneva's past and appeal.

TIP

As the holidays approach, the Lake Geneva Cruise Line creates a magical experience with its Santa's Hideaway cruise. Enjoy a 40-minute journey, concluding with a visit from Santa Claus himself.

Eat!

PAPA'S BLUE SPRUCE RESORT
W4086 Lakeshore Dr.
262-729-4126

MARS RESORT
W4098 S Shore Dr.
262-245-5689

GRANDMA VICKIE'S CAFÉ
522 Broad St.
262-249-0301

THE GETAWAY ON LAKE COMO
W4190 West End Rd.
262-686-3456

MEGGY MOO'S DAIRY RIPPLE
600 Kenosha St.
Walworth
262-394-5584

Stay!

THE BAKER HOUSE
327 Wrigley Dr.
262-248-4700

SEVEN OAKS BED & BREAKFAST
682 S Wells St.
262-248-4006

CASES TURN OF THE CENTURY BED AND BREAKFAST
N1599 Hillside Rd.
262-248-4989

to Do!

LAKE GENEVA CRUISE LINE
812 Wrigley Dr.
262-248-6206

YERKES OBSERVATORY
373 W Geneva St.,
Williams Bay
262-245-5555

BLACK POINT ESTATE AND GARDENS
W4270 Southland Rd.
262-248-1888

GENEVA LAKE MUSEUM
255 Mill St.
262-248-6060

THE CHEESE BOX
801 S Wells St.
262-248-3440

TOPSY TURVY BREWERY
727 Geneva St.
262-812-8323

Visit!

BIG FOOT BEACH STATE PARK
1550 S Lake Shore Dr.
262-248-2528

From Lake Geneva, head west on WI-50 W. Turn right on South Seventh Street. Turn left on WI-11, arriving in Delavan.

Lake Geneva Cruise Line

From its humble beginnings as a temperance colony to its flamboyant circus era and subsequent transformation into a resort destination, Delavan's stor is one of remarkable evolution. Founded in the early 19th century by th Phoenix brothers, Delavan was conceived as a haven for those seeking sober lifestyle. Their temperance ideals shaped the town's early characte influencing its architecture and social fabric. Yet fate had a surprising twis in store for this seemingly straight-laced community.

Delavan unexpectedly emerged as the winter home for numerous circu companies in the mid-19th century in a dramatic departure from its sobe origins. The town's proximity to transportation routes and abundant ope space made it an ideal location for circus troupes to rest and prepar for their annual tours. Delavan was a bustling circus metropolis fo nearly half a century, hosting iconic shows like P. T. Barnum' *Greatest Show on Earth.*

The circus era left an indelible mark on Delavan. It legacy can still be seen in the town's circus-theme personality. While the big tops have long sinc departed, the spirit of showmanship lives on.

As the circus era faded, Delavan's idylli surroundings took center stage. The clea waters of Delavan Lake, surrounded b rolling hills and lush greenery, prove irresistible to visitors seeking respite from cit life. The town gradually transformed into thriving resort destination, with a wide rang of recreational activities, from boatin and fishing to golf and swimming.

TIP

More than 250 members of the historic circus community found their final resting place within the sacred grounds of Spring Grove and St. Andrew's Cemeteries. Look for numbered plaques at their gravestones.

Romeo the Elephant greets visitors to Delavan.

to Do!

EAST TROY RAILROAD MUSEUM
2002 Church St., East Troy
262-642-3263

J. LAUBER'S ICE CREAM PARLOR
2010 Church St., East Troy
262-642-3679

THE ELEGANT FARMER
1545 Main St.,
Mukwonago
262-363-6770

WEBSTER HOUSE MUSEUM
9 E Rockwell St.
Elkhorn
262-723-7848

HISTORIC SPRAGUE THEATRE
15 W Walworth St.
Elkhorn
262-441-3924

Visit!

SPRING GROVE AND ST. ANDREW'S CEMETERIES
North Seventh St.

TOWER PARK
117 Park Pl.

Stay!

LAKE LAWN RESORT
2400 E Geneva St.
262-728-7950

MAIN STREET MANOR OF DELAVAN
112 S Main St.
262-740-0798

Eat!

JONATHAN'S ON BRICK STREET
116 E Walworth Ave.
262-725-7715

THE DUCK INN SUPPER CLUB
N6214 WI-89
608-883-6988

ANNIE'S BURGERTOWN
645 N Lincoln St.
Elkhorn
262-723-3250

GUS'S DRIVE-IN
3131 Main St.
East Troy
262-642-2929

WAGON WHEEL DELAVAN
2891 Co. Rd. O S.
262-725-6193

RIGA-TONY'S DELICATEZZI ITALIANO
5576 State Rd. 50
262-740-2540

FROM DELAVAN, head west on WI-11/ Walworth Avenue. Turn left onto County Road O. Turn right onto Beloit Avenue, which turns into South Main Street in Janesville.

JANESVILLE

Janesville possesses a blend of history and flavor, from the covert world of the Milton House to the timeless charm of the Cozy Inn Chinese restaurant.

The Milton House flourished during a pivotal period in American history: the Underground Railroad. Built in 1844 by Joseph Goodrich, the Milton House was designed as a stagecoach inn. However, its true significance lies in its role as a safe haven for those seeking freedom. Hidden within the Milton House complex is a secret tunnel connecting the main building to a nearby cabin. This underground passage provided a crucial escape route for enslaved people fleeing to the North. The house served as a place of rest, food, and most importantly, safety for those fleeing bondage. The Milton House presents a stirring connection to Janesville's past, allowing visitors to step back in time and understand the bravery of those on the Underground Railroad.

Eat!

COZY INN CHINESE RESTAURANT
214 W Milwaukee St.
608-754-9826

O'RILEY & CONWAY'S IRISH PUB
214 W Milwaukee St.
608-752-6099

BUCKHORN SUPPER CLUB
11802 N Charley Bluff Rd.
Milton
608-868-2653

FREDRICK'S SUPPER CLUB
118 Merchant Row
Milton
608-868-2966

BESSIE'S DINER
1716 W Airport Rd.
608-743-9830

The Lincoln-Tallman Museum

For a different kind of historical experience, consider visiting the Cozy Inn, which has been serving authentic Chinese dishes since 1922. As a culinary time capsule, it's the second-oldest Chinese restaurant in the US continuously operating from the same location. The Fong family, owners since 1974, have played a pivotal role in the Cozy Inn's legacy. Tom Fong, the current owner, recalls his childhood spent in the restaurant, learning the intricacies of the business from his mother. Their dedication to preserving the restaurant's history is evident in the meticulous care taken to maintain its original ambiance.

The nation's second-oldest Chinese restaurant in the same location

Stay!

CENTURY ELMS BED AND BREAKFAST
2200 W Memorial Dr.
608-751-2354

GUARDIAN ANGEL BED AND BREAKFAST
429 Prospect Ave.
608-758-3211

Visit!

NORTHSIDE BREWERY EXCAVATION
Across from Mercyhealth Hospital
1000 Mineral Point Ave.

TIP

The Rock Aqua Jays have held water ski performances on the Rock River for more than six decades. This 22-time national champion team delivers free shows from Memorial Day to Labor Day.

to Do!

LINCOLN-TALLMAN HOUSE MUSEUM
440 N Jackson St.
608-756-4509

STERLING NORTH MUSEUM
409 W Rollin St.
Edgerton
608-884-8337

MILTON HOUSE MUSEUM
18 S Janesville St., Milton
608-868-7772

BECKMAN MILL
11600 S Co. Rd. H, Beloit
608-751-1551

NORTHLEAF WINERY
232 S Janesville St., Milton
608-580-0575

DEVIL'S STAIRCASE TRAIL
Ice Age National Scenic Trail at Riverside Park

LOGAN MUSEUM OF ANTHROPOLOGY
700 College St., Beloit
608-363-2000

LEAVING JANESVILLE, take East Milwaukee Street headed east. Continue on East County Road A. Turn left on North Tarrant Road. Turn right on WI-59 E. Turn right onto West Whitewater Street in Whitewater.

Victoria on Main Bed & Breakfast

WHITEWATER

Whitewater is a titan in the world of Paralympic basketball. The University of Wisconsin-Whitewater's wheelchair basketball program has etched an indelible mark on the sport, serving as a breeding ground for Paralympic champions.

The program's roots stretch back to the early 1970s, when the university initiated adaptive recreation services. Wheelchair basketball emerged as a popular and competitive outlet, laying the foundation for the powerhouse program it would become. Decades of dedication and a supportive campus environment have cultivated an unparalleled legacy of excellence.

UW-Whitewater has produced a staggering number of Paralympic athletes. Their dominance on the national and international stage reflects the program's commitment to developing well-rounded athletes. The university's facilities and experienced coaching staff have created an optimal training ground for aspiring Paralympians.

Beyond the medals and championships, Whitewater's wheelchair basketball program has been a catalyst for inclusivity. By showcasing the extraordinary abilities of athletes with disabilities, the program has challenged stereotypes and inspired countless individuals. The university's commitment to providing opportunities for all students has made it a beacon of hope for aspiring athletes worldwide. As the Paralympic movement continues to grow, Whitewater's legacy as a powerhouse in wheelchair basketball will endure. The program's impact extends far beyond the court, leaving a lasting impression on the world of sports and disability rights.

TIP

Visit Whitewater's Flowing Well: a natural spring well that has steadily flowed since Adam Channing hand-dug it in 1895. Bring containers to take water home.

Eat!

BINGGS FARMSTEAD RESTAURANT
N416 Twinkling Star Rd.
262-203-9830

FANATICO
162 W Main St.
262-472-0747

BRAIN FREEZE
535 E Milwaukee St.
262-458-2334

WHINEYS WINE AND BEER HAUS AT THE FUZZY PIG
N8660 Clover Valley Rd.
262-473-4574

Visit!

STARIN PARK WATER TOWER
504 W Starin Rd.
262-473-0122

NATURELAND PARK
W8338 Territorial Rd.
262-741-3114

OLESON CABIN
N9156 Duffin Rd.

PIONEER LIME KILN
Near Nordic Skiing and Hiking Trails parking lot
N9084 Co. Rd. H

PARADISE SPRINGS NATURE TRAIL
W374 S8640 Co. Rd. N
Eagle
262-594-6200

BIRGE FOUNTAIN
402 W Main St.

to Do!

OLD WORLD WISCONSIN
W372 S9727 WI-67, Eagle
262-594-6301

THE FUZZY PIG
N8660 Clover Valley Rd.
262-473-4574

HANG GLIDE WISCONSIN
N463 Co. Rd. N
480-251-1515

Stay!

HAMILTON HOUSE BED & BREAKFAST
328 W Main St.
262-473-1900

EAGLE CENTRE HOUSE BED AND BREAKFAST
W370 S9590 WI-67, Eagle
262-363-4700

FROM WHITEWATER, follow Main Street US-12 BUS W. Take a slight right toward US-12 W. Turn right onto US-12 W. Continue straight onto US-12/North Main Street and Fort Atkinson.

FORT ATKINSON

Named after General Henry Atkinson, Fort Atkinson's origins are closely connected with the Black Hawk War of 1832. Established as Fort Koshkonong, a temporary military outpost, the area's strategic location at the confluence of the Rock and Bark rivers made it a vital point of control. After the war, the fort was abandoned, but the settlement that grew around it flourished.

One of Fort Atkinson's most enduring legacies is its link to the dairy industry—the Hoard family, pioneers in dairy journalism, established *Hoard's Dairyman* magazine in the city. The dairy industry flourished in Fort Atkinson, thanks in part to publications like *Hoard's Dairyman*. This publication became a leading voice in the industry, solidifying Fort Atkinson's reputation as a dairy center.

Another local giant, Jones Dairy Farm, has also contributed significantly to the city's dairy heritage. Founded in 1889 by Milo Jones, the company has grown from a small-scale operation into a nationally recognized brand synonymous with breakfast sausage. The Jones family's history is closely connected with the state's agricultural heritage.

Hailing from one of Fort Atkinson's founding families, Jones was the son of dairy farmers who had migrated from Vermont in 1832. His entrepreneurial spirit was ignited when he began selling his mother's homemade sausage recipe to friends and neighbors. The overwhelmingly positive response quickly transformed this hobby into a thriving business. The company's iconic farmhouse, still on the original farm site, symbolizes its long history and enduring family legacy.

Eat!

PADDY COUGHLIN'S PUB
14 Sherman Ave. W
920-397-7776

MANGIAMI ITALIANO
226 S Main St.
920-397-7790

SCOTTIE'S EAT-MOR
124 N Main St.
920-563-2900

WEDL'S HAMBURGER STAND & ICE CREAM PARLOR
200 E Racine St., Jefferson
920-674-3637

ROCK BOTTOM EXPRESS
211 S Gardner Ave.
Jefferson
920-675-1950

THE CORNER
718 S Main St., Jefferson
920-674-4033

BRICKHAUS CAFÉ
126 E Milwaukee St.
Jefferson
920-674-2015

Stay!

BARTEL'S BEACH COTTAGE
124 S Ferry Dr., Lake Mills
920-648-8421

Visit!

FORT ATKINSON WATER TOWER
S Fourth St.
and S High St.

TIP

Bring the whole family, including your furry friend, to the Jones Dairy Bar. It serves doggie cones and a fresh water bowl to keep your pup cool and comfortable.

to Do!

FIRESIDE DINNER THEATRE
1131 Janesville Ave.
920-563-9505

JONES MARKET
601 Jones Ave.
920-563-2963

HOARD HISTORICAL MUSEUM
401 Whitewater Ave.
920-397-9914

NATIONAL DAIRY SHRINE
401 Whitewater Ave.
920-863-6333

HIGHWAY 18 OUTDOOR THEATRE
W6423 US-18, Jefferson
920-674-6700

STABLE ROCK WINERY & DISTILLERY
123 W Milwaukee St.
Jefferson
920-541-3459

LEAVE FORT ATKINSON via North Main Street. Continue straight onto WI-89 N. Turn left onto US-18 W. Turn right onto WI-89 N. Turn right onto County Road Q. Turn right onto County Road A. At the traffic circle, take the second exit and stay on County Road A. Turn right onto Main Street in Watertown.

WATERTOWN

Watertown owes its existence to the power of the Rock River. Situated amidst rolling hills and fertile farmland, the city's history is intertwined with the industrial development of the 19th century.

Founded in 1836 by Timothy Johnson, Watertown's strategic location along the river provided ample water power for sawmills, grist mills, and other early industries. As the city grew, so too did its economic diversity. German immigrants, arriving in large numbers in the mid-19th century, brought their own cultural and economic influences, contributing to Watertown's rich tapestry.

Watertown holds a distinctive place in the history of education. It was within this small town that the concept of kindergarten was first introduced to the US. The visionary behind this groundbreaking endeavor was Margarethe Meyer Schurz.

TIP

Mullen's Dairy Bar has an uncommon tradition since 1932: when the mercury plummets to minus 20 degrees or colder, it serves free single-scoop ice cream cones.

Visit!

AZTALAN STATE PARK
N6200 Co. Rd. Q, Jefferson
608-873-9695

TIVOLI ISLAND NATURAL PARK
101 Tivoli Dr.

In 1856, Schurz, a German immigrant with a deep appreciation for the educational philosophies of Friedrich Fröbel, opened the nation's first kindergarten in her Watertown home. Her kindergarten was a radical departure from traditional schooling, emphasizing play, exploration, and social interaction as essential components of early childhood development.

Located behind the Octagon House Museum is America's First Kindergarten.

Schurz's innovative approach to education quickly gained attention, inspiring educators across the country to adopt similar methods. Her work laid the foundation for the kindergarten movement in America, and her legacy continues to shape early childhood education today. This groundbreaking educational initiative put Watertown on the map as a progressive and forward-thinking community.

Eat!

ZWIEG'S GRILL
904 E Main St.
920-261-1922

MAIN STREET CAFÉ
116 E Main St.
920-261-8760

HARTWIG'S WATERLOO DINER
111 N Monroe St.
Waterloo
920-966-0588

THE HUB
128 E Madison St.
Lake Mills
920-945-0090

LEWIS STATION WINERY, DISTILLERY & KITCHEN
217 N Main St., Lake Mills

Stay!

KATHERINE HOLLE HOUSE
119 N Church St.
920-253-2444

JESSE STONE HOUSE BED & BREAKFAST
300 S Washington St.
920-262-1918

to Do!

MULLEN'S DAIRY BAR—WATERTOWN
212 W Main St.
920-390-4606

AMERICA'S FIRST KINDERGARTEN
919 Charles St.
920-261-2796

KRAEMER WISCONSIN CHEESE
1173 N Fourth St.
920-261-6363

LITTLE AMERRICKA AMUSEMENT PARK
700 E Main St., Marshall
608-620-5224

OCTAGON HOUSE MUSEUM
919 Charles St.
920-261-2796

AZTALAN MUSEUM
6264 Co. Rd. Q
Jefferson

FROM MAIN STREET in Watertown, merge onto WI-16 E. At the traffic circle, take the second exit and stay on WI-16 E. Exit the traffic circle onto WI-16 E. Take the exit toward Oconomowoc. Turn right onto WI-16 E.

Visit with Dorothy and the gang in downtown Oconomowoc.

OCONOMOWOC

Although it's disputed, Oconomowoc boasts a storybook claim to fame: it's the place where the iconic film *The Wizard of Oz* premiered in 1939. To commemorate this historic event, the city created Oz Plaza, a magical space celebrating the classic movie. Located in the heart of downtown Oconomowoc, the plaza features life-sized statues of Dorothy, Toto, the Scarecrow, the Tin Man, and the Cowardly Lion. Visitors can follow a yellow brick road that leads to the center of the plaza, where they can pose for pictures with their favorite characters. The plaza not only honors Oconomowoc's connection to *The Wizard of Oz* but also adds a touch of enchantment to the city's downtown area.

After experiencing the magic of Oz Plaza, take a trip back in time at the Kiltie Drive-In. The drive-in, complete with a giant neon sign, serves up a classic Americana dining experience that perfectly complements the enchantment of downtown Oconomowoc. The Kiltie Drive-In has served classic eats with a side of old-fashioned charm since the late 1940s. Carhops glide effortlessly between parked cars, delivering burgers, hot dogs, and crispy fries on metal trays. The menu is a classic American diner affair, focusing on simplicity and quality. But it's more than the food that keeps customers coming back. The restaurant's retro atmosphere, complete with vintage signage and timeless tunes, creates a nostalgic ambiance that's hard to resist.

TIP

Built in 1907 with distinctive fieldstone, the Delafield Fish Hatchery represents Wisconsin's pioneering conservation efforts. This historic site replenished the state's lakes and streams with fish via electric railway.

Visit!

OZ PLAZA
168 E Wisconsin Ave.
262-569-2186

Stay!

THE DELAFIELD HOTEL
415 Genesee St., Delafield
262-646-1600

MON BIJOU
351 E Lisbon Rd.
262-315-4065

to Do!

HONEY ACRES
N1557 WI-67, Neosho
920-474-4411

STONE BANK FARM MARKET
N68 W33208 Co. Trunk Hwy. K
920-355-4021

KETTLE MORAINE STATE FOREST—LAPHAM PEAK UNIT
W329 N846 Co. Trunk Hwy. C, Delafield
262-646-3025

OCONOMOWOC HISTORICAL MUSEUM
103 W Jefferson St.
262-569-0740

Eat!

KILTIE DRIVE-IN
N48W36154 E Wisconsin Ave.
262-567-2648

MAXIM'S AT OCONOMOWOC DEPOT
115 E Collins St.
262-569-0072

PRIBNOW'S MAPLE INN
N887 WI-67, Ixonia
920-474-7527

KUHTZ GENERAL STORE FOOD & SPIRITS
W335N6939 Stone Bank Rd.
262-966-2142

BELFRE KITCHEN
606 N Genesee St., Delafield
262-303-5066

REVERE'S WELLS STREET TAVERN
505 Wells St., Delafield
262-646-4070

WINE MANIACS WINE BAR & BISTRO
114 N Main St.
262-244-0385

RED CIRCLE INN
N44W33013 Watertown Plank Rd.
Nashotah
262-367-4883

INDEX

9781681065809.